PLAY BETTER SQUASH

by John Beddington
of Lambton Squash Club, Kensington, London

A PLAYFAIR PUBLICATION

Diagrams by Tony Matthews

Published by The Queen Anne Press Limited,
12 Vandy Street, London EC2A 2EN.
Printed by Hazell Watson & Viney Ltd,
Aylesbury, Bucks.
Photoset by Seventy Set Ltd, London.

between the international and American versions of the game, he arranged a tournament at his own club in which leading players competed under the American scoring system (for good measure, he also devised an 'all-play-all' format, familiar in the Masters tennis tournament but highly unusual in squash). That is the kind of thing John Beddington gets up to. His wide-ranging interests have made him a director of the Lambton Squash Club (North Kensington), which was born in 1972 and is now expanding into an international company; European tennis consultant for Commercial Union, who back the Grand Prix circuit and its climactic Masters tournament; and the Tournament Director of the BP International Tennis Fellow-ship.

That in the midst of all this he has found time to write a book on squash is at once both remarkable and typical. During its preparation he discussed the technique of stroke production with the elegantly facile Sajjad Muneer, a superb striker of the ball. The bulk of this volume concerns tactics and technique, but there is also much solid information and sensible comment on wider areas of the game. The author is always good company and his readers will benefit from the advice of a kindred spirit. They may also find future comfort in the fact that, if there are no squash courts in the next world, John Beddington will cer-ainly build some.

CONTENTS

FOREWORD

by Rex Bellamy
Tennis and squash rackets correspondent of *The Times*; author of *The Tennis Set*; joint author of *Teach Yourself Squash Rackets*

A long association with tennis and squash has, among other advantages, granted me the privilege and pleasure of a close acquaintance with three congenial JBs: John Barrett in tennis, Jonah Barrington in squash, and John Beddington in both. All are energetically imaginative and have a rare capacity for opening windows in the mind. John Beddington, the author of this book, is the least well known of the three because his talents have primarily been exercised on the periphery of the courts rather than in the spotlight of personal publicity. But his relatively modest status as a player is, as it happens, a recommendation to those who are about to enjoy his book; he is writing mainly for his would-be peers in the higher echelons of squash, for those who are facing, or are about to face, the kind of challenges he has met and mastered himself.

He was never taught squash, but picked up the game and subsequently reached a high level as a club player competing for BP in the Cumberland Cup and Cool competitions. That is probably more than most of us will achieve. But it represents a standard to which reasonably aspire if they have the ambition, ability and character. This book will help them on the way because it is by a man who understands their problems and is young enough to share them. In the past years author not only at his own club (a relaxed players at every level) but also, by a bizarre circumstances, at Salem in Massachusetts made sympathetic allowance for the years. It is equally relevant that his American squash indicates an unquenchable game, no matter where or how it may

His restless spirit of enterprise ment in January, 1974. In an at

INTRODUCTION

So you want to play squash? Well, this book has been written not only for the beginner learning to play for the first time, but also for the player who has been hitting the ball around for some time and wants to improve his present standard.

For the beginner the first sight of a squash court may be daunting. The view from the gallery is of a more or less square, gleaming pit with wooden floor, white walls and ceiling, no windows, and apparently no door. The first sight of squash being played may, of course, be equally disconcerting – two men dressed in white shirts, shorts, shoes, and socks running wildly to and fro whacking a little black ball around the walls with alarming enthusiasm.

However, the beginner can quickly appreciate the enjoyment to be gained from the game. The physical activity, the need for fast reflexes, and the concentration and anticipation make squash a superb fun and exercise game. For the more advanced player, improvement will bring ample opportunity for tournament and championship match play at all levels, from club ladders and leagues to international status.

It has been said that becoming a champion is, like genius, the result of 90 per cent perspiration and 10 per cent inspiration. Squash is a game that exercises both the mind and the body, so that any effort to improve needs to be both mental and physical. However, to become a real champion at the game, the perspiration will be more of the mind than the body. Physical fitness is vital, but it is a small matter by comparison with the mental effort the average player must make for consistent improvement.

The popularity of squash has increased beyond all expectation during the past few years, largely because it is a game suitable for both men and women of all ages – from those still at school to those approaching, or even well into, middle-age. It has also become the most cosmopolitan game of our time.

Traditionally, books on sport are written by experts, for example, Rod Laver on tennis, or Jack Nicklaus on golf. This book is about squash – what the game is and how it is played.

Above all, it is a game to be played with enthusiasm – and in that respect this book is written by an expert. Although there are countless squash players who are better than I am, there are few who take more pleasure in the game.

ACKNOWLEDGEMENTS

Inevitably there are many people to whom an acknowledgement should be addressed with reference to this book. Equally inevitable is the fact that they cannot all be mentioned.

Knowledge gained in any subject, especially in a sport such as squash rackets, is the result of many years' experience, both on and off the court – mine is no exception. I have been lucky enough to meet many people interested in the game, including the world's top players, administrators, entrepreneurs, and enthusiasts. Most of these friends and acquaintances have contributed to this book, however indirectly, for my knowledge of and enthusiasm for this superb game have been increased by contact with them.

I have received invaluable advice from my wife Roseann, who does not play squash but who has patiently and laboriously typed the manuscript, improving it in the process. For practical and technical assistance I am indebted to Sajjad Muneer of Pakistan and Philip Carling at Lambton Squash Club. I should also like to thank my partners at Lambton, Mark Vere Nicoll and Colin White.

I am indebted to Rob Jolly and Alex Angeli, editor and publisher respectively of *The Squash Player* international magazine, for kindly supplying the photographs in the centre section. For those readers who wish to learn more about the game and keep abreast of current developments, *The Squash Player* is highly recommended as one of the best sports magazines of its kind available. I am grateful to Rob Jolly for his assistance with the biographical section as well.

I should like to thank the SRA for their permission to reproduce the rules of the game, and Peter Woods, the secretary, for his unfailing assistance. I should also like to thank John Horry, former secretary of the SRA and now secretary of the International Squash Rackets Federation, for his help.

I am indebted to the players, too – Jonah Barrington, Geoff Hunt, Ken Hiscoe, Gogi Alauddin, Hiddy Jehan, John Easter, Cam Nancarrow, Bryan Patterson, Mohammed Yasin, Abbas Kaoud, and many others. I have watched and learned from all of these fine players when they have played at Lambton, and

9

have tried to transmit some of their technique and skills to the reader.

Last, but not least, I thank Rex Bellamy, who writes so fluently for *The Times* on squash and tennis, for his foreword. Rex is a keen squash player and is co-author with Leslie Hamer of *Teach Yourself Squash Rackets*.

Part One

1 SO YOU WANT TO PLAY SQUASH?

It had taken a lot of persuading. After all, James had not taken any form of exercise for three years and it had begun to show. His muscles, once proud and taut, were in an early stage of flabbiness and his waistline was not quite what it used to be. Not quite a paunch – he was only 28 – but perhaps his friends were right. Squash might be the answer for him. It seemed to be popular with many people.

James's real problem was not fear of fierce exercise but fear of being ineffectual, which would severely damage his pride. In his earlier years he had kept quite fit and managed to be fairly competent at athletic games, but he would be a complete beginner at squash. Some of his friends at the office had played for years and their enthusiasm, to say nothing of their apparent fitness, was daunting. He did not particularly relish the thought of losing to any of them.

But the fight had been won. One cold winter's night James found himself setting off for his first game of squash. He had searched around in his wardrobe and found his old tennis shoes which had turned a distinctive yellow. He added a white holiday shirt and some white football shorts that were very tight round the waist, and he was off, both nervous and excited, yet at the same time pleased that he had finally made the effort.

The squash club was pleasant and comfortable and his opponent greeted him cheerfully, with no hint of embarrassment at the strange assortment of sports gear that appeared from James's bag. James was not completely ignorant of the game – he remembered that it wasn't very different from tennis in some ways. One player serves, the other player returns, and the rally continues until one of the players makes a mistake. Instead of being on opposite sides of the court, squash opponents must share the same confined space, and instead of hitting the ball 'over the net' it must be hit above a line on the front wall of the court. Squash couldn't be too difficult as it therefore consists of hitting a ball around in a four-walled room. Shots must be easier to make, as it is quite difficult to hit a ball out of a four-walled room – in tennis it is easy to send it too far or too wide.

James's opponent kindly lent him a squash racket, and he soon found himself on court about to begin the knock-up. His friendly opponent had chosen a very slow ball and James was somewhat taken aback to find that it hardly bounced at all – it merely plopped against the wall and refused to return to the back of the court. But James was quick to learn that the ball must be warmed up, and that the best way to do this is to hit it as hard as possible at the front wall. So, with a swing of the racket and on flat feet, James began. He was pleasantly surprised at how simple it seemed to hit the ball at the wall, and, having realised that the wall is a vast area offering a great margin for error, he began to find squash less frightening. However, he had already begun to make mistakes that would be harder to rectify the longer they persisted.

James soon found that being able to hit the ball, he could begin to play a game. A quick discussion of the basic rules and the determination of someone who hates to lose soon enabled him to perform with reasonable competence. At the beginning, the pace of his improvement was his greatest encouragement; but after a while, although his enthusiasm remained and the will to practise strengthened, nothing more was achieved in terms of progress. It was at this point that James realised that he had improved as much as possible on his erratic beginning to the game and if he was going to improve any further he would need help. Furthermore, he was going to have to unlearn some of the faulty techniques he had developed.

Where could he go for help? Coaching is available from several sources, but is often expensive and inaccessible. However, a few books exist on the basic technical approach to the game – this is another one! The mere idea that a book can teach anyone to play a game is debatable, but many fine sportsmen as well as ordinary club players use books and articles to learn more about their own sport.

Squash is one of the obvious games to be learnt from a book for two very good reasons. It is not a difficult sport to begin, as James discovered, and there seems little reason why it should be a difficult sport to learn *correctly* once one has begun. Simple instructional passages on the basic strokes can be easily followed and put into practice. The other principal reason stems from the extreme shortage of qualified professional coaches; the game has expanded so fast that the increasing demand for coaching at all levels has far exceeded the supply of coaches. Consequently the majority of beginners must learn the first steps with the aid of a book.

Looking at the state of another increasingly popular game, golf, one beginner seeking professional advice on how to take it up was told to find a 'basic swing', and then practise for six months before venturing on to the course. There is much to be said for this type of advice if the player in question has the determination of an Olympic athlete. Unfortunately most beginners have not, and so this book is not aimed at Olympic athlete types. The desire to improve is tempered by an eagerness to play matches. To be locked on a squash court for six months until one can hit the ball with unerring efficiency is perhaps the quickest way to improve, but it is certainly not the most enjoyable.

Play Better Squash aims to help the beginner, whatever his ambitions, to play properly right from the start. He can still play matches and it is hoped that he will; but if he follows the instructional sections, he will adopt the correct techniques and tactics in a simple progression, until he finds to his great surprise that he is playing good squash. That is not to say that poor James has been left in an anguished plight. The book will show him his errors, and on the strength of his own ability he will be able to rebuild a sound platform from which to improve.

That is what learning a new game means – the building of a sound technique that will not falter whatever the stresses and pressures applied to it. Allied to this comes a basic understanding of what can be achieved and of what the player is trying to achieve, whether during a particularly close game or during his career as a whole. It is hoped that this book will be of value not only to the beginner or to the moderate player; for if by its very simplicity it reminds the better player of some of the fundamentals of the game of squash, then it will be of help to him also.

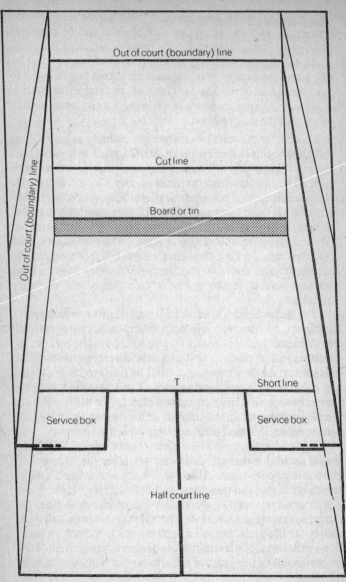

Out of court (boundary) line

Out of court (boundary) line

Cut line

Board or tin

T

Short line

Service box

Service box

Half court line

Diagram 1a The court: definitions.

The Game of Squash Rackets

The game of singles in squash is played between two players. One player serves the ball from one of the two service boxes on to the front wall above the service or cut line and below the boundary line, so that it rebounds into the opposite back quarter of the court behind the short line and on the other side of the half-court line. The server is known as *hand in* and the receiver is known as *hand out*. The right to serve at the beginning of a game is decided by the spin of a racket.

After the server (hand in) has served, the receiver (hand out) can return the ball by hitting it after it has bounced on the floor, or on the volley before it bounces. Whichever option he chooses, the ball must be returned, without bouncing on the floor either directly or by way of one of the other walls, to the front wall above the board or tin.

From that point, players hit the ball alternately and play continues until one of them fails to make a good return. This can happen if he does not reach the ball before it bounces on the floor for the second time, or if he hits the ball below the board into the tin or above the boundary line on any of the four walls. It is also possible to lose a point by standing in the path of an opponent's ball if it would have travelled directly to the front wall after he has hit it.

If a player has been hand in and loses a rally, he loses the right to serve and the hand out receiver becomes hand in as server. Points can be scored only by the server, and if a rally is won by the receiver, the serve changes hands but no point is scored.

The first player to reach nine points wins the game unless the score reaches eight-all. If this happens, the receiver has the choice of playing one more point or two, to nine points or 10. Thus a game can be won 10-8, 9-8, or 10-9, depending on this choice. Matches are usually the best of five games, the winner being the player who is first to win three games.

This is a brief summary of how squash is played and the further you read the more you will understand. A beginner will soon notice the attractions of the game: plenty of exercise in a short period and in a fairly limited area; unlike tennis or badminton, the margin of error in hitting the ball out of court is considerable – it is therefore easier to keep the rally going and requires less basic skill to be able to play at all; squash can be practised on your own without the absolute necessity of a partner or opponent (improvement is also more likely to follow from practising alone as far as technique is concerned); squash is invigorating.

Squash does not damage your ability or skill in other sports such as tennis. There are several very good tennis players who are also more than just proficient at squash, for example, Ken Rosewall and Roger Taylor. Both use squash as a training ground for tennis, since it requires similar reflexes, breathing, speed, accuracy, and coordination.

Now let us move on to the technical requirements of the game.

Equipment and Clothing

Apart from the basic necessity of a court in which to play, the equipment and clothing required for playing squash can be readily obtained at any reasonable sports, or club professional's, shop. Finding a court is less easy and, when located, they are usually heavily booked in advance. A list of affiliated clubs in your area can be obtained from the Squash Rackets Association, 70 Brompton Road, London SW3 1DX. The whereabouts of public courts can usually be obtained from the appropriate local authority.

The basic equipment for squash is a racket and ball; the basic clothing includes shirt, shorts, socks, and shoes. Women can replace the shirt and shorts with a dress suitable for sport or a shirt and skirt. These items need not be expensive and you may find that you already have some of them if you play tennis. One important fact to remember is that the rules of the game stipulate that all clothing should be white. The reason for this is that a black ball can be sighted more easily when crossing a white surface. Some people feel that the all-white rule may be changed in deference to colour television but it is expected that this will be only for televised play, if at all.

The Racket

The choice of a racket depends on the individual, who must first decide upon the price range he can afford. Racket prices vary enormously, and for the beginner a modestly-priced one is quite sufficient. The head of the racket must have a wooden frame but the shaft may be made of wood, metal, cane, or even glass-fibre.

The important point to remember about choosing a racket is that it should feel comfortable – the weight and the balance must suit the individual. The grip on the handle is also a matter of personal choice, and may be either towelling or leather. Towelling grips have a shorter life but are inexpensive and easily replaceable. They are recommended for those who find leather grips slippery. One can even buy rackets with grips moulded to the pattern of the hand so that the beginner is sure to hold the racket in the correct way.

It does not matter to the beginner if the racket is strung with gut or synthetic fibres. However, experienced players may find that rackets strung with gut provide more control. (Nylon and other synthetic strings have a longer life, are cheaper and more easily obtained, while gut strings become scarcer and as a result more expensive.) The racket should be treated carefully, particularly if strung with gut. Do not leave it with wet clothes as the gut will fray quickly in damp conditions. It is not essential to use a press with modern rackets, a plastic headcover being quite satisfactory. The racket should be left in a dry and cool place.

If you are to play in a match and some of the strings in your racket are slightly frayed, it is better to have the strings repaired beforehand, rather than having to interrupt the match when a string breaks. One other point to remember; however good or expensive a racket is, it will not last any longer than any other if it is hit hard enough against the walls or the floor.

The Ball
The ball and the racket are both defined in the final section of this book.

In the United Kingdom, there are four types of what is basically the same ball – blue dot, red dot, white dot, and yellow dot. The blue dot is the fastest and the yellow dot is the slowest. It is the yellow dot that is used in tournaments and competitive events.

The speed of the ball varies not only because of its own specification but also on account of the type of court on which it is used. On a hot court the air inside the ball warms up with the result that the ball moves off the walls faster. Therefore, it is obviously better to use a slow ball on a fast or hot court, and a faster ball on a slow or cold court.

Apart from using the type of ball most suitable for the court on which you are playing, it is generally easier for the beginner to start with a fast or blue dot ball.

Shoes

There are many different varieties of shoe that can be used for squash, but a basic white canvas one with a good gripping sole is quite satisfactory as long as it is strong enough to cope with the pressures put on it by constant twisting and turning. The shoe must not have black soles which will mark the court's surface.

When buying shoes, bear in mind the thickness and number of pairs of socks you will wear.

Socks

It is most important that your feet feel comfortable when you are wearing socks and shoes, otherwise you will not be able to concentrate on your game.

Some players wear no socks, while others wear one or even two pairs. It is usually advisable and comfortable to wear some, but however many pairs you wear depends on your individual comfort. If your feet blister easily then you may prefer to wear two pairs, though usually one thick pair is enough. The prime importance is comfort.

Always wear a clean pair of socks each time you play; apart from anything else, dirty socks cause blisters more easily. Look after your feet – wash and dry them carefully after playing; and use foot powder if you feel it necessary.

Shirt, shorts, skirts, dresses etc

These clothes should be white, easily washable, and, most important, comfortable. They should not be too tight or too loose, or restricting in any way.

Other Equipment

Other useful items for the squash player include a towel, which is essential and should be available outside the court for use between games.

Towelling wristlets can be useful for the player who finds sweat pouring down his arms an unnecessary danger to a firm grip on the racket.

Sweatbands came into use originally to aid the player with glasses. Fewer people play in glasses now that contact lenses are available, but sweatbands are still useful for keeping long hair under control.

A wide variety of sports bags are available in which to carry your clothing and equipment.

It may seem unnecessary to go into such detail on equipment and clothing as much of what has been said may seem obvious. However, it is necessary to stress the importance of these aspects of the game and also how preferable it is to have your own. Keep it in good condition and turn up on court looking well prepared in clean clothes. The advantage in doing so may be psychological – but it will be an advantage nevertheless.

The Court

How the size of a court became standardized is described in 'The state of the game'. The standard dimensions of a squash court are defined in the last section of the book. However, there are still many courts that have not been built to the standard international dimensions. These are either relics of the time when there was no standard specification for a court, or those which have been built since then without due consultation with the experts.

A court is basically 32 feet from the back wall to the front wall and 21 feet across. The diagram on the next page shows the dimensions. The walls of the court should be white and constructed of a special type of hard plaster which has to contend with considerable wear and tear.

The floor should be well sprung and ideally made of maple, but other strong timber, such as pine or birch, may be used. However, the floor must not be treated with too much seal; this will make it very slippery, because sweat will not be absorbed, and dangerous accidents may be caused.

The board or tin (or 'tell-tale' as it is sometimes known) is set at the bottom of the front wall, and should have a small cupboard set into it in which to place wallets, watches, handbags, and other valuables during a game.

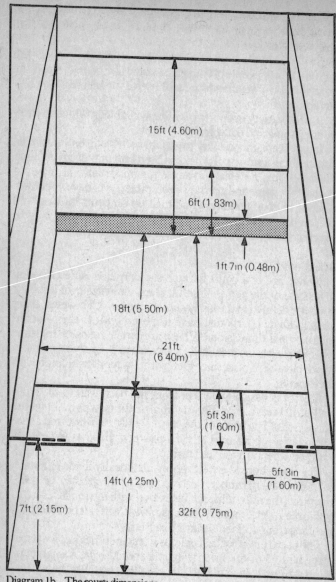

15ft (4.60m)

6ft (1 83m)

1ft 7in (0.48m)

18ft (5 50m)

21ft (6 40m)

5ft 3in (1 60m)

5ft 3in (1 60m)

14ft (4 25m)

32ft (9 75m)

7ft (2 15m)

Diagram 1b The court: dimensions.

The ceiling should have a clearance well above the specification in the rules and a minimum of 19 feet is suggested for good squash. Also, the lights should not hang down so far that they will impede high shots but should be set high in the ceiling to illuminate the court brightly and evenly.

A gallery is not imperative, but is useful for spectators. If the court is a cold one, some form of heating in the gallery is recommended as squash can otherwise be an extremely cold game to watch.

One important aspect of any squash court or set of courts is ventilation. Without proper ventilation, walls will sweat and condensation will form.

These are just a few points about the court which may serve as a guide. However, the business of constructing a squash court is highly technical and, if you are ever considering it, you must seek advice from the experts at the SRA. Short cuts in construction are usually a false economy, since mistakes can be very expensive to rectify. If the builder is unfamiliar with court construction, check with the SRA on plans and construction materials. The SRA will also be able to guide you on the best types of floor or plaster and so on.

2 ELEMENTARY STROKES

The Grip

At this stage, we must assume that you are familiar with the basic principle of squash. There are two players on the court and you are taking turns at hitting the ball and in so doing trying to frustrate the efforts of your opponent in making a good return (without actually standing in his way). Thus, reduced to simplicity, your object is to strike the ball against the front wall and cause it to bounce twice on the floor before your opponent can produce a reply to your shot. If you do that you win a point, and if you do it often enough you will win enough points to win the game, and eventually the match.

Your shot will be made either as a defensive measure against your opponent's attack, or as an offensive measure to put your opponent on the defensive. It is important that you should understand this distinction now, because once you are on court playing, the difference between the two will be forgotten while you are more concerned with the problems of reaching the ball and hitting it effectively.

It is important to emphasize that learning to strike the ball correctly on both the forehand and backhand sides is absolutely essential. There are no short cuts and practice is the only way to achieve a satisfactory and fluent consistency of stroke. So the first thing to learn is how to grip the racket properly, in order to be able to hit the ball most effectively. Squash is a game that demands a high degree of efficiency; consequently you must ensure that the first step is an entirely correct foundation on which to build your game. If you are a beginner and you do not learn to grip the racket in the right way at the outset, it will be extremely difficult for you to readjust later.

However, every squash player, being human, is different – there are no two Jonah Barringtons or Geoff Hunts – and you must allow your own natural tendencies to be moulded into your style of play, so that you do not limit your horizons. This individuality applies to the grip as much as to the rest of your game. We will show you the conventional grip here but players with unorthodox ones have been known to be equally successful.

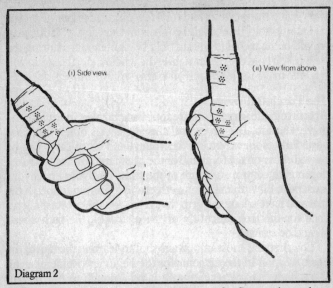

(i) Side view   (ii) View from above

Diagram 2

The grip. Note that (i) the thumb is placed between forefinger and second finger, while (ii) the V between thumb and forefinger is almost central on the handle.

With the first purposeful wrapping of the fingers round the racket handle comes your initiation into the wonderful game of squash. Take the racket in your left hand (if you are right-handed) and hold it vertically by the shaft with the racket face facing sideways. Extend your right hand to 'shake hands' with the racket handle, and settle your thumb and forefinger round it with the 'V' on top. The palm of the hand is slightly behind the handle and the other fingers are spread round it to give support and solidity. The thumb should extend round the handle, ending up between the forefinger and the second finger. Some experts prefer to advise gripping the handle like a hammer, and if you prefer this then the forefinger should meet the thumb round it (but on the inside).

The 'V' formed by the thumb and forefinger should be almost central on the centre line of the shaft of the racket but slightly to the right. The racket should be held as near to the base of the handle as is comfortable.

Once you have settled your hand round the handle in this

23

way, swing the racket round for a few minutes to get the feel of it. Do not hold it too tightly – it is not necessary. Your grip should be relaxed and should only be tightened for hitting the ball. If you hold the racket tightly the whole time, the strain will begin to make itself felt and your arm will tire more quickly.

The Forehand Drive

Apart from the serve there are four basic strokes in squash: the drive, the lob, the drop, and the angle. All other shots are variations of these (except the volley) and all of them can be played either on the forehand or the backhand. On these strokes depends the entire structure of the game and your endeavour must be to hit with maximum effect and minimum effort. Now that you have adopted a grip that gives you the greatest allowance for the free execution of these strokes, the path ahead should be easier.

The first and most important shot to learn is the drive, the basic weapon in the armoury of the beginner. Remembering from James's experience that it is not enough to hit the ball hard, you must learn to hit it with consistency and control, qualities more important than sheer strength. This is also a good moment to mention what may seem obvious – keep your eye on the ball. Many mistakes are made by average players who do not watch the ball right on to the racket.

The drive can be divided into three parts; backswing and preparation, impact, and follow-through. With your left foot forward and your feet at right angles to the side wall, you are standing parallel to the course of your shot. Your weight should start on the right foot as you raise the racket on the backswing to a point just above and behind your head. The elbow should remain bent and the wrist should remain cocked so that the racket head is held up vertically.

Your knees should be bent at this stage as you will be able to move the weight of your body more easily from right foot to left foot. The more weight you put into a shot the more powerful it will be. Swing the racket down from the backswing position above and behind your right shoulder and simultaneously shift the weight of your body to the front foot, keeping the knee bent for balance. Strike the ball at a point just opposite your front foot and parallel to the front wall, keeping your shoulders

Diagram 3

The forehand: (i) backswing (ii) impact (iii) follow through.
Note that the weight is transferred from right foot to left.

square to the side wall. Be careful not to let your shoulders turn until the ball has been struck and your follow-through has begun. If your shoulders open towards the front wall before impact the ball will tend to fly off across the court instead of up and down. This usually stems from a desire to hit the ball too hard and should be avoided until you have worked your forehand drive into a well-grooved stroke.

The racket should follow through continuing its arc to a point above the left shoulder, with the elbow slightly bent so that the racket stays close to the body.

The action of hitting the ball is similar to throwing one. Although the wrist should remain cocked during the backswing, it may be lowered for the moment of impact depending on the height at which the ball will be struck.

You should learn the forehand and backhand drives with the racket-face square to the front wall; do not attempt at this stage to use spin, or to cut the ball, as mistakes can easily be made. It is more important to become proficient at the basic strokes before learning sophisticated variations.

Diagram 4

The backhand: (i) backswing (ii) impact (iii) follow through.
Note that the weight is transferred from left foot to right.

The Backhand Drive

To many beginners, the backhand stroke may seem more difficult than the forehand, but this should not be so – after all, it is
easier to throw a hat at a hat-rack with a backhand swing rather
than a forehand. Beginners who spend more time practising the
supposedly more difficult backhand often end up with a more
fluent and correct stroke than on the forehand, where the initial
swing at the ball may tend to prevail because it has met with
reasonable success. The backhand is an instinctive stroke.

The basic ingredients of the backhand drive are similar to
those of the forehand, except that the ball falls on the player's
opposite side. For instance, if the player is right-handed and the
ball falls on his right as he faces the front wall, he will play a
forehand; if it falls on the left, he will play a backhand. As
squash is played within walls it is not often possible to run
round a backhand and hit it on the forehand as can be done in
tennis or badminton.

Once again it is necessary to emphasize that the proper execution of the stroke should be learnt. The wrist and the forearm

should follow a sweeping arc down from a high but compact backswing, with the arc from left to right. There should be no inward turning of the wrist.

As the racket sweeps down to the ball, the moment of impact corresponds to the moment at which you let go of the hat towards the hat-rack, and is similar to slapping with the back of the hand. However, the fact that the backhand is more instinctive than the forehand does not mean that you will necessarily end up with a stronger backhand stroke. Each individual player will use his own method, adapting the textbook stroke. This is merely to show you the ease with which you will be able to pick up the technique for the backhand.

Thus the stroke itself will start from above the left shoulder with the weight on the back (left) foot. The wrist remains cocked and the racket head up, with the right shoulder at right angles to the front wall. Maintain a well-balanced stance while you transfer your weight to the front foot as the racket begins its sweep down to the ball, smacking the ball level with the front foot as the full weight of the body reaches that foot. The knees remain bent and the racket follows through with elbow slightly bent, to keep the racket close to the body.

The Crosscourt Drive

As we have said, the basic forehand and backhand drives just described are the first and most important in a player's armoury of strokes. The straight drive should be played up and down the court parallel with the side wall until you have a well-grooved stroke and swing. When you have practised this on both flanks and feel you have mastered in part the essentials of timing and technique, then we can look at the next stage of the drive – across the court.

The crosscourt drive from the forehand side should be made in a similar way to the forehand drive down the wall. With the front foot forward and the knees bent you should swing the racket back, bending the elbow, and 'throw' the racket at the ball hitting through it. The moment of impact should be in front of the left foot so that you hit the ball early by comparison with the drive down the wall. It is better to keep the racket face open for the crosscourt stroke unless you wish to 'kill' the ball, in which case you will take it at the height of its bounce,

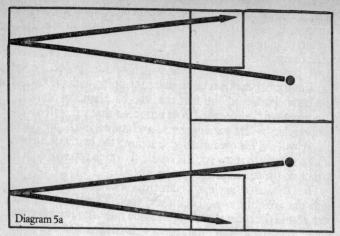

Diagram 5a

Straight forehand and backhand drives.

Crosscourt forehand and backhand drives.

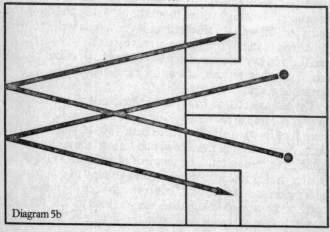

Diagram 5b

28

stroking down and across. If you do not want to hit the ball in the early position, the same shot can be effected by changing the position of the body so that it is parallel to the path of the stroke you are about to make.

The backhand crosscourt drive should be played in the same way as the forehand but from the left side of the court hitting towards the right. Crosscourt strokes can be used to deceive the opponent – and the art of making your opponent think the ball is going to be hit in a different direction plays a big part in squash. By shaping up for a forehand or a backhand drive, you can hit down the wall or across court merely by changing the moment of impact very slightly. If you hit the ball opposite the front foot it will travel parallel to the body, if you hit it just in front of the front foot it will travel across the court.

Simple Practice

This is your first introduction to tactics and at this stage it will be useful to look at some fundamental points. Nobody can learn the straight drive and the crosscourt drive merely by reading a book. It is not even enough to go and play a match in which you make some effort at following the basic principles. Winning is the object of any match, and it is an important part of the psychology of winning that you do not experiment with technique once the match has begun – so the only answer for real improvement is plenty of practice.

Squash can easily be practised on your own and the best way to make sure that you understand what you have read is to go into a court and practise the strokes in the same order in which you have read about them. But don't practise for too long or you may become bored.

Initial practice sessions should be taken easily and it is advisable not to try and do too many things at once. Play the ball up and down the side wall so that it bounces in or about the service box. Practise the shot until you feel you have coordinated all the necessary technique, and then practise a little more until you begin to hit every ball into the service box.

A good drive is the result of a ball hit at the correct pace and height. To take this one stage further, the most important drive is the one that is hit down the wall to bounce well before the back wall, with the second bounce dying on the back wall. The use of the wall is important, as we shall see in the next section, to prevent your opponent from being able to cut the ball off before it passes him to land at the back of the court.

The length of the drive is an important element in the effectiveness of the shot. If the length is good your opponent will only have one chance to hit it and that is before it passes him. It should not bounce off the back wall to give him a second chance. If the shot is close enough to the wall then your opponent may also be unable to stop the ball before it passes him.

In practising, the whole height of the front wall should be used to gauge the power and direction of your shots. The higher you hit the ball at the front wall, the softer it should be, but you can hit harder as you aim lower towards the tin. If you practise with this in mind then you will soon learn that you do not have to hit the ball too hard all the time. Concentrate all the time while you are practising, for bad practice is worse than none at all.

Practise the crosscourt shots in the same way – aim to hit the ball into the service box area to begin with, and then extend this by aiming to land the ball deep into the far corner from where your opponent will have difficulty in retrieving it.

This elementary tactic of trying to keep the ball away from your opponent will be discussed more fully together with other simple tactics later in this chapter under the heading *Basic Tactics*. Before we get to that stage we must first have a look at the service and the return of service.

The Service

As every point must begin with a service, you cannot do more than practise without it. It is therefore the only shot which is played in every rally, and it must be included in this chapter before you begin to play a game of any kind.

There are players at all levels who do not pay enough attention to the art of the service. Being the only shot in the game that is not a return of your opponent's shot, you are not in any sense under pressure. You should not consider it as just a method of putting the ball in play and starting a point. It is a good opportunity to put your opponent under pressure even though it is extremely hard to gain a point outright with a service winner.

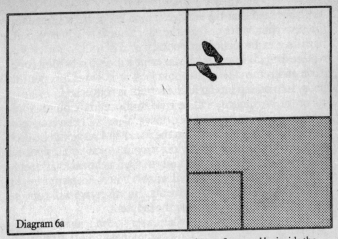

Diagram 6a

The forehand service from the right court: only one foot need be inside the box. The shaded area shows where the ball must bounce.

The forehand service from the left court: the left foot is nearest to the front wall. The shaded area shows where the ball must bounce.

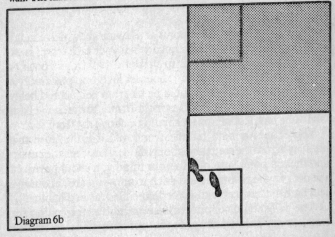

Diagram 6b

Having seen that the service can and should be used as an offensive shot, you must use the advantage it will give you. As we will see in the section on tactics, the art of squash is to be able to place the ball where your opponent will find it hardest to retrieve and return. We must now look at how we can put this theory into practice as far as the service is concerned.

For the beginner it will be wise to concentrate on the forehand service from both service boxes. Nearly all players prefer the forehand service although the backhand serve can be used to good effect if only to vary the way in which your opponent has to receive it. There is certainly a case for the backhand serve in the forehand court – this will enable you to keep your eye on your opponent and his movements. However, we will concentrate on the forehand serve for the moment.

There are two principal types of service in squash – the lob and the hard service. The most common and most effective of these (if correctly hit) is the lob, which we will look at first.

Don't forget that you have plenty of time – use it to position yourself correctly. The left foot should be in front of the right, whichever side you serve from, and should be nearer to the front wall. You can stand with either one or both feet in the service box but you will save yourself some movement after you have served if you stand with only one foot firmly in the box. Diagrams 6a and 6b show the ideal position of feet for the forehand serve. Dig your feet in solidly and stand well balanced.

The ball can be hit at any point of the wide arc which extends from your feet to above your head when your racket arm is extended. However, it is better to strike the ball from a position somewhere between knee and shoulder level and preferably at about hip level. The ball should be hit from behind and below in an upward arc which will carry it firmly towards the front wall. The moment of impact should be above the front foot.

You should aim to hit the front wall a little more than halfway across the court and about midway between the cut line and the top boundary line. In your mind you should mark off the area on the front wall at which to aim – an area about four feet high and six feet wide is recommended (as in diagram 7).

The ball should continue to rise, as high as the ceiling permits, on its journey towards the opposite court and should

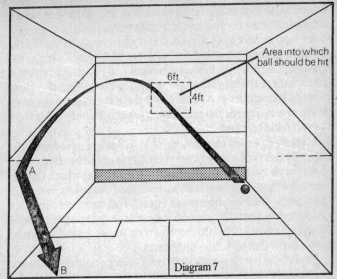

Area into which
ball should be hit

6ft

4ft

A

B

Diagram 7

The lob service: the ball, hit from the service box, should rebound from the front wall on to the side wall (at A, approx. 4-5ft from the back wall), and then bounce (at B) before striking the back wall.

glance off the side wall on its downward path at a point equidistant from the back wall and the floor – preferably between four and six feet. Height is important, as the higher the ball goes in the arc after hitting the front wall, the more vertically it will drop in the far corner. The aim of the lob serve is to keep the ball so close to and high on the side wall that your opponent cannot volley it before it drops.

The ball should drop after hitting the side wall and bounce before hitting the back wall. The only way for your opponent to return this type of serve is by digging it out defensively which keeps you on the offensive and well placed.

Thus the lob service is a carefully hit lob aimed to drop as deep as possible in the far corner without your opponent being able to make a good return. If the ball hits the side wall and then the back wall before bouncing it will be forced out into the centre of the court, where your opponent can return it with interest; so try not to overhit the service, or to hit the serve too low so that your opponent can reach it to volley before or after it hits the side wall. You must also avoid hitting the side wall too early as that will bring the ball out into the court as well.

As soon as you have served you should move to the T, the junction of the half-court line and the short line. This is the commanding position in a squash court and you should attempt to reach there before your opponent. (See the section on simple tactics.) Remember one thing about the lob service – no power or speed is required, just technique, which can only come from considerable practice.

If your opponent seems to be able to read your serves satisfactorily then you should vary them. This could be the time for you to try a backhand serve to alter the angle at which the ball comes off the front wall. The occasional variation in service may catch your opponent off guard, and surprise can often produce dividends. If your opponent is caught out of position he may have to do a block return or move in the opposite direction to that which he intended.

One of the best ways to catch your opponent in this way is to throw in the occasional hard service, the other principal type of serve. This should be hit from a similar position to the lob service. The ball should be hit flat and aimed hard just above the cut line; it should stay close to the side wall, hitting it close to the floor. The length of the shot should be good, i.e. the second bounce should die on the back wall.

The principles of serving outlined here apply equally to a serve from either side of the court.

Before moving on to the return of service, let us look briefly at the requirements for a service as far as the rules of squash are concerned. When serving, at least one foot must be completely inside the service box (not touching the red line) and the ball must be hit between the cut line and the boundary line on the front wall. Hitting the lines in squash is 'out' and therefore the ball must hit between those two lines. If you do not have one foot completely in the service box it will be counted as a fault. If the ball hits the wall on or below the cut line but above the tin it is a fault; however, your opponent may accept this service by returning it in the normal way which negates the fault.

The ball must also land in the opposite back quarter of the court (the shaded area in diagrams 6a and 6b). If it does not land in that quarter it is also a single fault, but your opponent may accept it by returning it. If you have served a fault, you are allowed another serve but you can only serve twice in this way on each point. Your opponent may also volley the serve before it lands in his quarter.

Double faults are served if you hit the ball on or above the boundary line or on or below the tin on the front wall and also if your serve never reaches the front wall. It is also a double fault if the ball is served and hits the ceiling or the boundary line (or higher) on any of the other three walls. A double fault also occurs if the server serves two single faults, or if he fails to strike the ball at all while attempting to serve. Finally, it is a double fault if the serve touches one of the side walls before the front wall.

Return of Service

After a service, the receiver must return the ball on to the front wall above the tin. Like all other shots, the ball must not touch his body or clothing and must not be hit twice. Unlike the service, the return may hit a side or back wall on its journey to the front wall, where it must land below the boundary line and above the tin. If it does touch a side wall it must do so below the boundary line.

The object of explaining to you how to return the service is simple. It may not be as easy as a straightforward drive and it is important that you learn how to tackle the service from the receiver's point of view. After all, if your opponent has learned how to serve the lob service and rarely makes a mistake, you must quickly learn how to retaliate.

As the receiver, you are under pressure from the server, whose prime objective is to make things as difficult as possible for you. He is under no pressure and has the initiative, which you have to try and gain from him by placing the ball as far away from him as possible. After serving he will have moved to the one position which dominates the court – the T. From that point the furthest place on the court is one of the corners.

The first thing to learn is where to stand so that you have the best chance to return service adequately. In diagram 8, you will see that you should stand in the back corner near the centre line. From there you can look sideways towards the server and determine the type of service with which he will be presenting

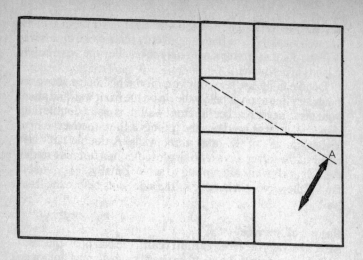

Diagram 8

Receiving service: in left court *above*, in right court *below*. Stand at A, facing the side wall but looking over your shoulder (along dotted line) to determine the type and direction of service. Once the ball has been struck, move forward (along arrowed line) to cut it off on volley if possible.

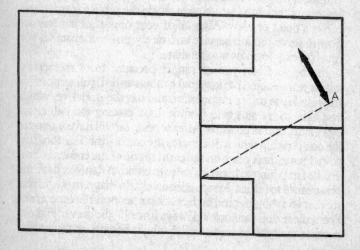

you. As soon as he has struck the ball, you can anticipate where it is going and if possible cut it off on the volley before it lands along the back wall or in the corner. Move from your receiver's position in a line towards the nearest corner of the service box.

The ball has to land in the receiving quarter, and working on the principle that it is easier to move forwards rather than backwards, you should not stand anywhere other than position A to receive. From there you can quickly move forward to any part of the receiver's quarter.

The safest return of service is a straight drive parallel to the side wall in your quarter, hit to a good length. This can be either a drive after the ball has bounced or, preferably, a volley. Equally successful is a lob, driven or volleyed, along the side wall to a similar length. Both these shots land in the back corner and force your opponent to move from the T towards the back of the court, leaving the T position vacant for you.

Variation is obviously desirable in returning service. However, it is vital that you master the safe returns before attempting more advanced and sophisticated shots. The other safe return is a crosscourt lob into the far corner. To be successful this shot must have plenty of height and should be kept as wide of the T (and therefore as near to the side wall) and as deep as possible. In both cases this is to avoid your opponent. These are the two principal safe returns and remember, 'when in doubt, play safe'.

If you decide that your opponent's serve is not formidable, as soon as you have determined the ball's direction there are three basic offensive strokes you can employ to give you the initiative. The straight drop shot to the front corner nearest to you and the crosscourt drop shot to the far front corner are both difficult shots to play with accuracy, but may provide you with the means to move your opponent up the court while you gain the T position. Both shots need much practice. They can be played either on the volley or after the ball has bounced.

The third attacking stroke from this position is the reverse angle boast. You hit the ball first on to the far side wall from where it will rebound on to the front wall above the tin and drop back on your side of the court quite far up in the front corner. The service off which you hit this shot will need to have bounced away from your side wall to enable you to get the racket behind the ball.

If a service is very good, then almost certainly the only means of return will be defensive and the use of the boast will be necessary. The boast is a shot that touches a side wall before reaching the front wall. A good service may prevent you from getting the racket sufficiently behind the ball to hit it straight down the side wall. In this case you will have to aim it at the side wall at such an angle that it will rebound on to the front wall above the tin (preferably close to the far front corner). By using this shot you can turn a difficult situation into an advantageous one by once again forcing your opponent into one of the corners. See diagram 9c.

The boast return should be hit in the same way as a drive but the racket face should be sufficiently open to carry the ball across the court to a point above the tin; the point of impact should be between the body and the side wall.

top right Offensive returns of service: (i) straight drop shot (ii) crosscourt drop shot (iii) reverse angle.

below Safe returns of service: (i) straight drive or lob (ii) crosscourt lob.

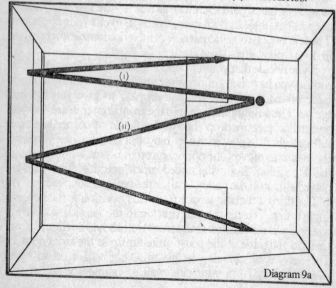

Diagram 9a

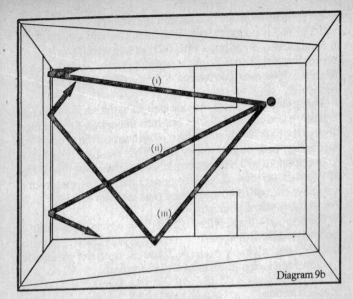

Diagram 9b

below Defensive return of service: boasted shot.

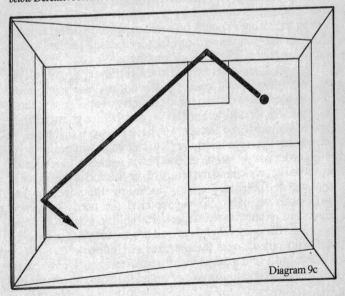

Diagram 9c

As your proficiency at squash increases you can move forward to receive service, provided that you still cover all the possible areas. Standing a yard further in may help you to return services more easily on the volley but it may also force you to step sideways or backwards occasionally to dig out a good service.

If a service glances off the side wall on to the back wall before bouncing and the ball comes out into the centre of the court, always try to back up and return it without turning round and hitting the ball on your other side. This can be dangerous as your opponent will almost certainly be within your line of fire. If you back up towards your opponent without turning round, you have the added advantage of pushing him off the T as he has to move out of your way.

Remember – if a service is difficult to return, play a safe or defensive shot. If it appears to be easy, play an attacking shot, but keep the ball away from the T and the centre of the court.

Now for a look at the basic tactics of squash.

Basic Tactics

With the forehand and backhand straight drives as the bread and butter shots of squash, your first attempts at practising hitting the strokes should be concerned with correct timing. Once you have mastered the timing, everything else will follow including power. Timing is all important.

This book has so far been written as if every squash player was right-handed. Of course this is not the case but as most players are, I have catered for the majority. I apologise to those left-handers who have read so far and before going further, would venture to suggest that you have already found it easy by now to interpret the instructions to suit your own game.

In order for you to be able to play a game we have already covered the service and the return of service and in the course of looking at these basic shots (including the forehand and backhand) we have also encountered the need for tactical discipline on court as well as technical ability. The lob, the drop shot, and the boast (angle) have all been mentioned as well and a more detailed look at these strokes will follow.

One must first assume that the strokes already covered are within your repertoire as a player and that you can put the ball

40

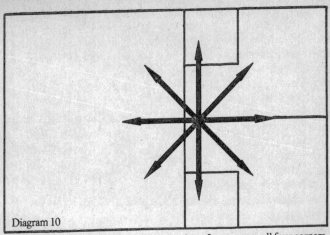

Diagram 10

Command of the T position: from here you have fast access to all four corners of the court.

roughly where you want it with those strokes. When you are completely proficient in stroke production and technique the game of squash becomes entirely a game of tactical manoeuvre.

There are two basic principles which must become instinctive on the squash court. The first is to dominate the T position and the second is to keep the ball as far away as possible from your opponent.

If you can learn to dominate the T position you will always have your opponent under pressure. The T (the point where the half-court line meets the short line) is the one position from which you can move fastest to any of the four corners. As soon as you have hit the ball, you should immediately move back to the T to prepare for the next shot from your opponent. Don't stand and enjoy your own stroke, however perfect, as you will lose valuable moments.

You should never let the ball out of your sight; watching your opponent, or better still, his racket, will give you a valuable clue as to the probable direction of his next shot. As soon as the ball is hit, you will be able to react faster if you have already anticipated its direction from watching how your opponent hit it. Be on your toes and move with the ball after he has played his stroke.

41

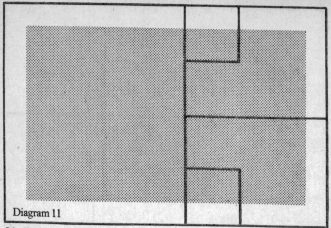

Diagram 11

Ideally, keep the ball out of the shaded area, i.e. the centre of the court.

As it is your earnest intention to command the T position, it may also be in your opponent's mind to do the same. If he manages to get there first, it follows that the second most important lesson in tactics is to keep the ball away from your opponent and away from the centre of the court and the T in particular. If you let your opponent get to the T and you don't keep the ball out of his reach, he will send you to all corners of the court making you use up valuable energy. You must not let him gain a position in which he can control the rallies.

Diagram 10 shows how easily your opponent, if he is on the T, can control the entire centre area of the court. One step takes him to within striking distance of the side walls and the areas in which a weak return may land. In order to keep the ball away from him when he is on the T, you must hit shots that do not land in the centre of the court. They must land within two feet of the front, back, and side walls, forcing him to move out of position.

Always hit to a good length if you can. It does not matter how hard the shot is, provided that it lands in the right place – within a short distance of the back wall, preferably in one of the corners. A perfect length for a drive occurs when the ball does not bounce a second time; instead it hits the back wall and drops forward on the floor so that no racket can scoop it up.

42

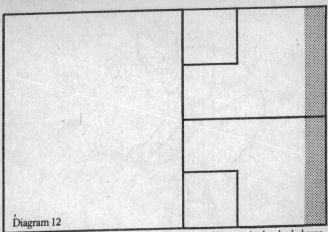

Diagram 12

A good length straight drive should have its second bounce in the shaded area.

When stepping on to the court for a game or match you always start by knocking up and getting the ball warm. You should hit the ball as you would in a game – don't relax just because there are no points to be won. If you usually hit the ball hard, then hit the ball hard. Find the rhythm of your game immediately so that when the match starts you know how to adapt it. Don't waste the knock-up; use it to get into the right frame of mind and to loosen the muscles. Your efforts will immediately give you an advantage and enable you to play the game your way.

Don't allow your opponent all the shots he likes in the knock-up. Just as you are trying to establish your authority, he will want to do the same. So if he likes hard drives and volleys, don't give him any. Let him do his share of the work to keep the knock-up going. Don't actually keep the ball away from him – merely send him the sort of shots you think he would find hard to play so that you have the advantage when the game starts.

Tactics should always be varied from day to day so that nobody can feel that they have a psychological advantage over you because they can anticipate your tactics. For instance Mohammed Yasin, victor over Jonah Barrington and finalist in the 1974 Benson and Hedges British Open Championship, has never beaten fellow Pakistani Gogi Alauddin, and try as he may

43

Diagram 13

The correct stance at the T – knees bent and racket ready.

he cannot find a way to win – Gogi is too smart a tactician. Yasin appears to be resigned to losing to Gogi – and the same can happen at any level of the game.

Tactics should never be the same, not only to keep your opponent guessing but also to take account of the speed of the court, the ball, the opposition, and of course, how you feel. Adapt your tactics to suit the conditions.

We have already seen the tactical purpose of the lob service – to hit the ball too close to the side wall for your opponent to volley and too deep in the corner for him to dig it out effectively (if at all). We have also seen the tactical returns of service that can be employed to make your opponent move from the T. Shots to the back corners will draw him away, and shots to the front will help him expend energy provided they are close enough to the side walls and do not bounce out into the centre of the court.

In discussing tactics and the T position, this is also perhaps the moment to mention the correct stance while at the T. Standing straight up with your racket trailing will not help you

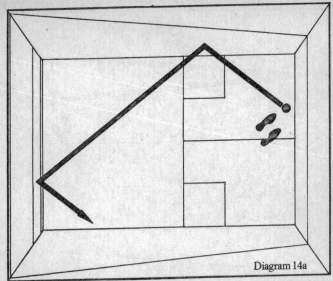

Taking the ball off the back wall: if there is not much room to manoeuvre, boast the ball off the side wall on to the front wall.

if you have to make a fast move. Therefore bend your knees, keep your wrist cocked with your racket head up, and remember that it is easier to move faster when you are on your toes, slightly stooping to give yourself extra 'leap' potential.

The need to command the T position is now firmly in your mind and you are aware that correct positioning on the court will result in your having to cover surprisingly short distances (compared to an opponent who never succeeds in reaching the T).

When taking the ball off the back wall, you should either face the back wall or the side wall. Give yourself room to hit the ball – don't stand too close to the spot where you expect it to bounce. It may come off the back wall direct from the front wall, or indirectly via a side wall. Only a ball that is a perfect length need beat you.

If the ball lands close to the back wall and does not allow much room to manoeuvre you will have to hit it sideways and upwards, boasting it off the side on to the front wall. However, if you are restricted to the back of the court like this, try and hit

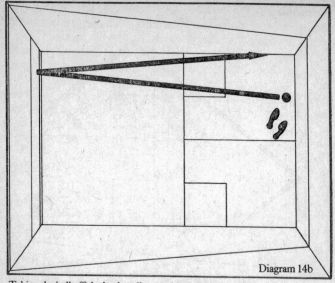

Diagram 14b

Taking the ball off the back wall: try to hit the ball straight to the near back corner off the front wall.

the ball straight to the near back corner off the front wall (see diagram 14b).

In moving to the T position, be careful not to get in the way of your opponent if he is attempting to return the ball from behind you. If he hits you with a ball which would otherwise have gone straight to the front wall the point is his – and you are probably very sore. A squash ball travelling at speed can hurt like hell! If the ball would have hit the side wall before the front wall then the point is replayed – but it still hurts.

One last point in this chapter. If an opportunity arises and your opponent gives you a shot off which you can hit a winner, go for it but try not to muff it. In order to achieve that position you have probably worked the ball and your opponent up and down the side walls until an opening was created (possibly by throwing in a short ball to keep him guessing). If the opening looks good to you, go for the winner. If he manages to scramble it back, you still have him under pressure and nothing is lost. But don't miss it or put it in the tin – not after all the effort you have put into that one point.

Summary

Before moving on to the remaining important strokes, it is worth pausing for a moment to sum up this chapter.

You have learned how to grip the racket and play forehand and backhand drives up and down the side walls and across court. You have learned how to serve and to return serve. You have learned some basic tactics and the value of simple practice. Here is a short list of points to remember – if you always bear them in mind, you may have an advantage over the next man.

1 Always watch the ball – even on to your opponent's racket. (Don't stare at the front wall waiting for his shot.)

2 For perfect stroke production, remember the importance of correct positioning of the feet.

3 Prepare early for your shots. Hold the racket cocked at all times so that the backswing is both easier and quicker.

4 Don't stand and admire your elegant drive, but prepare for the next one.

5 Get to the T and keep control of it.

6 Keep the ball away from the centre of the court and your opponent.

7 Vary the play. Always keep your opponent guessing.

8 Adopt the correct stance at the T, bending the knees and holding the racket ready. You are then ready to pounce on your opponent's stray shots.

Become proficient in these basic principles and you will have a foundation on which to build and develop a sound game.

3 FURTHER STROKES

The Lob

We have looked at the basic strokes and must now look at slightly more advanced, but nonetheless essential, strokes in any squash player's armoury.

When you enter a squash court and hit the ball for the first time, it is natural to hit it from below, bringing the racket from behind in an upward path. This, in its most elementary form, is the basis of the lob, which can be used as an attacking shot to win points or as a defensive shot to get out of a difficult position or to give yourself breathing space. The versatility of this shot makes it important.

The ideal lob will land in almost exactly the same place as the lob service – i.e. it will come off the side wall on its falling trajectory and will bounce before hitting the back wall close to the corner. The difference between the two shots is that the lob service must be hit from the service box, whereas the lob can and should be used from anywhere in the court. Thus, the ideal lob is one which is hit crosscourt to make use of the side wall to slow its pace before dying away right at the back of the court.

To play this shot the ball should be struck from below up towards the front wall, so that it rebounds further upwards and travels in an arc to fall as vertically as possible. Unless you are positioned close to the front wall, the ball should hit the front wall about or above the cut line but at least four feet below the boundary line. If you hit above that area you will find the ball will either go out (hitting the ceiling or roof) or have insufficient power behind it to carry it to the back of the court.

However, power and pace are not necessary elements of the lob. The most important factor is accuracy, as you only need to hit the ball firmly enough and at the right angle for it to rebound off the front wall to the back of the court.

The basic stroke for the lob is therefore the same as for a drive on either side, but the backswing should be substantial and the ball should be struck at a point in front of the front foot. The racket head may be allowed to drop below the wrist for this shot if necessary. The footwork is the same as for other shots, with the front foot forward; but the racket face should be open

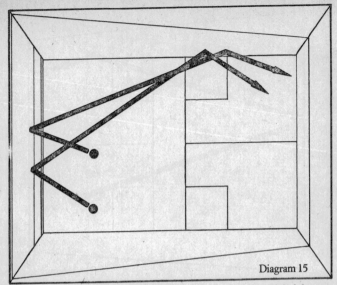

Diagram 15

Lob from front of court: ideally this should be crosscourt. A straight lob must be of a good length and avoid the side wall above the out of court line.

to lift the ball on its upward path to the front wall, and the ball should be hit from below. Hit the ball firmly – a mis-hit lob will either be volleyed fiercely if it is short, or it will come out into the court where it can be dealt with more easily if it is too deep. If you choose to hit the ball late, you will need plenty of wrist action to scoop it up.

In spite of being unspectacular, the lob is a most effective way of breaking up an opponent's rhythm and can give you great satisfaction – particularly if your opponent is so beaten by it that he can only stand and watch without any attempt at a return.

The object of the lob is to hoist the ball over your opponent so that, with luck, a weak return will be produced. Meanwhile you can take over the T position he has had to leave. The crosscourt lob is most effective as it makes use of the side wall to slow it down. The straight lob, while staying close to the side wall, must also be of a good length but can be more easily volleyed as the margin for error is even smaller than the crosscourt

49

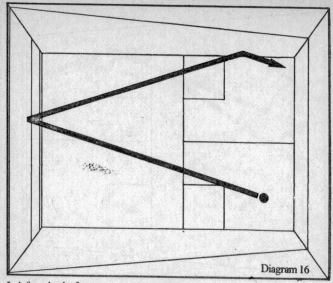

Diagram 16

Lob from back of court: crosscourt backhand.

shot. The boundary line on the side wall must be avoided which usually means the ball must fly nearer the T position.

Be careful before you start lobbing that you have mentally taken in the height of the ceiling or the lights. It is no use hitting an otherwise perfect lob if you find that on that particular court the lights hang down and your lob hits one. All courts vary in height.

As the lob can be used so effectively for both attack and defence, you should practise it from all parts of the court. It can be hit from either side after the bounce or even on the volley. It is also possible and often necessary to play a boasted lob – i.e. a lob that hits first the side wall and then the front wall before rising over your opponent to the back of the court.

Remember a good lob is always a safe shot. Whether played offensively or defensively, it can always become an attacking shot by virtue of moving your opponent from the T into the back corners.

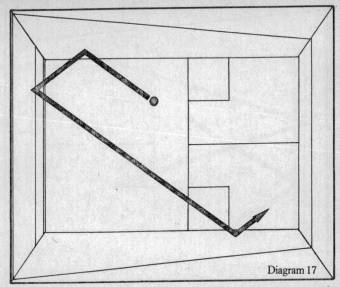

Diagram 17

Boasted lob: after hitting the front wall, the ball rises over your opponent and lands at the back of the court.

The Volley

The volley is the stroke that cuts the ball off in the air before it has a chance to bounce. When you consider how much the ball is in the air and how frequently it is possible to hit it before it touches the ground, you will realise how important the shot can be.

The volley is basically an attacking shot – with it you are able to dominate the game by not allowing your opponent sufficient time to recover. The volley is also an alternative means of returning the ball to the drive or any other shot from further back in the court. Rather than let the ball travel to the back of the court and possibly create problems, because you then have fewer means of return at your disposal, you cut it off by taking it early. This does not allow your opponent any chance to dominate the front of the court.

Keep the racket head up, as the time available for backswing may be limited. The volley is a short punch with a reduced backswing and a short follow-through. The basic shot is similar

51

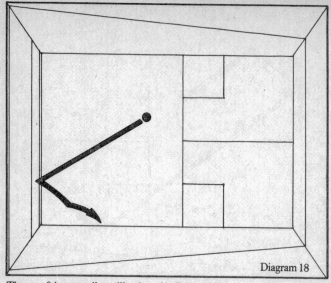

Diagram 18

The use of the cut volley will reduce the distance between bounces so that the ball will 'die' more quickly.

to the ordinary forehand and backhand strokes with the point of impact level with the front foot for the straight volley, though this can be varied according to the direction you wish the ball to take. The volley action, on either forehand or backhand, is a movement of the wrist and arm – you do not need to put your whole body into the shot. It is more of a quick reflex action than any other stroke in the game.

The volley can be used in any part of the court to great advantage, e.g. the return of service, but it is most effective as an attacking shot when you are positioned in the forecourt. Striking the volley from this position will produce many winners for you if you aim just above the tin and, preferably, close to the side wall so that the ball dies away in the nick.

The volley needs a lot of practice. Many players find the forehand volley easy but make mistakes with the backhand volley above shoulder level. It is entirely a question of practice, timing, and correct positioning as well as strength in the forearm and wrist.

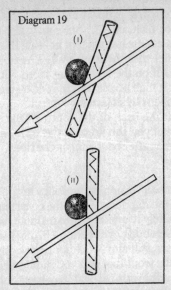

Diagram 19

(i)

(ii)

(i) Use of cut on the volley (ii) use of slice on the volley.

The volley is a key shot in top squash – the more you can volley, the more you can dictate the pace of the game and save yourself a great deal of running, as well as putting your opponent under constant pressure.

To hit volleys correctly from in front of the short line you should go forward as you hit the ball, having the backswing already in position (with the wrist cocked) and keeping your eye on the ball. Maintain your balance on the front foot (if necessary use your other hand to balance the body). Aim to strike the ball in mid-air at a point that is neither too ambitious to reach nor too low for you to be able to place your racket behind the ball. The shot can be hit with a slightly open racket face to reduce pace, or straight with a closed face to kill the ball.

The use of cut on the volley can be usefully employed as it will bring the ball down from the front wall at a more severe angle and will shorten the distance between the first and second bounce. However, before learning how to cut the ball on the volley or any other stroke, learn the basic shots and be proficient in their use. The cut is executed by using an open racket face and by bringing it down and across the ball to impart underspin. (See diagram 19.) Slice may also be used on the volley – with the same motion, but holding the racket face vertical and parallel with the front wall. The effect is similar. If you find yourself on the wrong foot faced with a volley, play safe; either hit it high across the court or up and down the side wall using an open racket face for control.

If you are at the back of the court, all the same principles apply except that you should treat the volley as a drive struck before rather than after bouncing on the floor.

The Smash

The smash is also a version of the volley and is used to prevent an opponent's lobs landing deep in the court. In order to smash correctly and safely it is necessary to maintain an open stance so that you have flexibility of direction – in other words, when you reach up you can still aim for either front corner. The weight should be on the front foot and you should bend your back to give the shot extra whip, as you may have only a short backswing. Hit the ball well in front of you, down and towards one of the front corners, and follow through fully but carefully avoiding your opponent.

The Drop Shot

The drop shot can be played on either flank like all the other principal strokes, but produces more winners and more mistakes than any other. The drop shot is a winner if executed correctly; if not, the ball will either be set up for your opponent or in the tin.

The drop shot should nearly always be played from the front of the court, i.e. in front of the short line. Greater accuracy is possible the nearer you are to the front wall, but the principal reason is to avoid your opponent. You should only consider a drop shot if your opponent is behind you, for if he is in front, it would be senseless to give him a ball which is nearer him than you. There is one exception to this – it is often possible to play an effective drop shot from the back of the court down the side wall. Don't attempt to hit a crosscourt drop shot from behind your opponent until you have convinced yourself in practice that you can not only do it but that it will be a winner.

Diagram 20

Forehand drop shot. At this stage you are still in a position to deceive your opponent, i.e. you could play a drop shot, or a drive to either side of the court.

The action for the drop shot should begin with a full backswing to deceive your opponent into expecting a drive, a lob, or any other shot for which the backswing is the same i.e. except for volley or serve. You must bend your knees and get down to the ball which should be struck at the height of its bounce – with the racket parallel to the floor and the wrist cocked. You must strike the ball firmly but softly (or else it will come out too far into the court) from behind and slightly below. The racket face should be open and the ball should hit the front wall only an inch or two above the tin before rebounding towards the side wall. The perfect drop shot is the ball that rebounds from the front wall into the nick (the join between the side wall and the floor).

The positioning of the feet for this shot should be the same as for the drive – the front foot forward etc. – and the ball should be struck just in front of the front foot on to which the weight of the body should have been transferred at the moment of impact. The body should be well balanced to enable you to strike

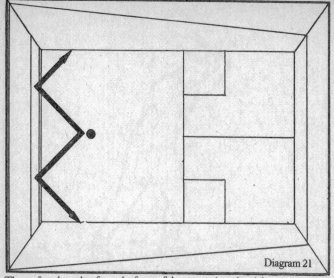

The perfect drop shot from the front of the court – into the nick.

firmly but softly through the ball with a short follow-through.

The shoulder should point towards the corner into which you are aiming the ball. If the ball does not go into the nick, it is better that it hits the side wall before bouncing on the floor. This will slow it down and keep it further away from your opponent.

The best time to go for a drop shot winner is when you are at the T and your opponent is behind you, having made a return that has come out into the centre of the court. Your drop shot should be towards the corner furthest away from him so that he has to travel the longest distance and expend energy in doing so. In addition it moves him right up the court, leaving it open for you.

The drop shot is sometimes used after you have run fast to reach the ball, tempting you to hit it hard. However, anticipate this and move with calculated strides towards the ball so that your balance is perfect at the point of impact. This will help you maintain control of the ball.

Thus, the drop shot can be played straight to the nearest side wall (diagram 21) or crosscourt (diagram 22). You hope that

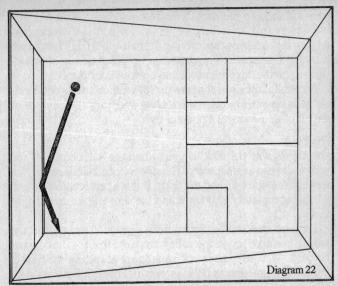

Diagram 22

Forehand crosscourt drop shot.

Drop shot from back of court: can be volleyed as a service return.

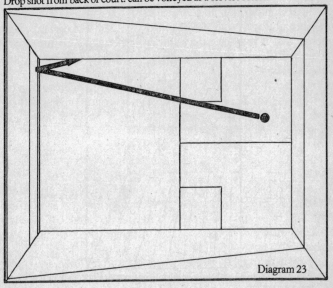

Diagram 23

both will land in the nick. The drop can also be played as a stop-volley (e.g. on return of service) which is a block shot, holding the racket out and giving the ball a short downward jab so that it loses pace. The drop can be sliced or top-spun depending on the circumstances and on your confidence.

Tactically, the drop shot is a useful weapon to use occasionally to keep your opponent guessing and vary the rhythm of play. It often produces a point or two.

The Nick
The expression 'the nick' is used when the ball comes off the front wall at an angle towards the side wall and lands in the join between the side wall and the floor. If it is a perfect nick the ball will fail completely to bounce and the shot will be an outright winner.

The nick shot can be played from a ground stroke (after the ball has bounced) or on the volley, from the front of the court or the back. Whatever happens, an attempt at hitting the nick if you are in a position to do so is worthwhile; if it fails as a nick shot, the ball will rebound off the side wall but stay close to it

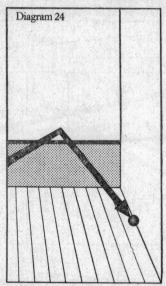

Diagram 24

The nick: when the ball lands at the join of floor and side wall, failing to bounce – it 'dies'.

and lose pace from contact. The nick is the best possible way to end a rally. A well-executed and successful nick is a most satisfactory shot and will boost your morale while reducing your opponent's.

Control and timing and choice of occasion must be perfect. As you play, you should be well balanced and well prepared with your racket at the ready position. From the front of the court, be sure you can play the shot you want – you will probably need a weak return from your opponent so that you are sufficiently well-positioned to go for the nick.

If you decide to go for the nick from the front of the court, do so when your opponent is behind you and deep in the court as if your timing is slightly wrong this will still be a difficult shot for him to reach. Start the backswing early, and keep it short. Keeping your eye on the ball, your weight should come forward on to the front leg and you should strike the ball with an open racket face in front of the front leg and follow through briefly. The knees should be bent. The action in this part of the court is similar to the technique for the drop shot – of which the nick is

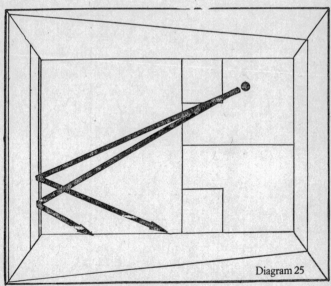

Diagram 25

The nick shot from the back of the court.

the most important type.

The nick can also be played with great effect from the back of the court although here there is a far smaller margin for error. The ball should be struck as for a drive, but not hit fully with normal driving pace. The crosscourt drive that lands in the nick is one of the finest shots in the game, but it is also one of the hardest to execute correctly. Hours of practice must be put in before you can ever play it with regularity – let alone under pressure from an opponent in a match.

4 ANGLES

During the course of previous chapters the subject of angled shots (or boasts, as they are known) has cropped up several times in explaining the fundamental points of stroke technique and the use of the various strokes. A boast or angle is a shot that is hit indirectly to the front wall; in other words, it is a return that strikes one or more of the other three walls first before hitting the front wall.

Angles deserve a chapter to themselves; not only can they not be considered elementary, but also a full understanding of angled shots and practical expertise in their use can convert an ordinary player into a mature tactician.

The use of the angled shot is one way to take advantage of the squash court's four walls. Whereas the basic drives up and down the court are the strokes on which your game is founded, the angled shot is more sophisticated and can bring infinitely more variety into play. The squash court is a specific size (21 feet wide and 32 feet deep) and you should learn to use every inch of it to move your opponent around and place the ball in positions which are as awkward as possible.

Apart from using the angled shot for this purpose, it can also extricate you from difficult situations. Very often, a shot hit to the back of the court is impossible to drive because you cannot move your racket round it to put enough power into the shot. The answer is to boast the ball off the side wall on to the front wall. This is a defensive measure and can be done in two ways. For a drop shot or nick, you aim for the ball to come off the side wall and travel across the court to hit the front wall in the far front corner; or you can skid-boast the ball, hitting upwards and forwards against the side wall, with the ball then hitting the front wall above the cut line fairly close to the centre and flying on upwards to glance off the other side wall and down into the back of the court. After the ball has hit the first side wall, it should travel a path similar to that of a lob service or crosscourt lob.

It is an ideal shot to play when you are stuck at the back of the court with your opponent on the T, being forced to play defensively. The value of the angle shot is that it can be played

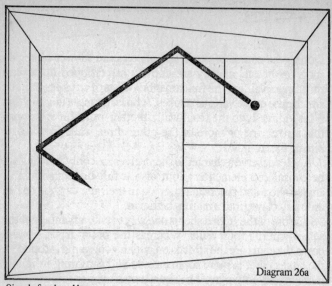

Simple forehand boast.

Boasted crosscourt drop shot.

Diagram 26a

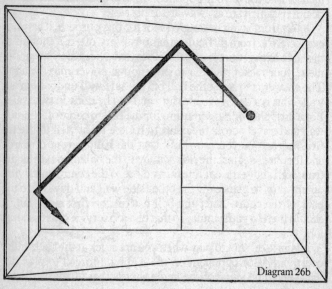

Diagram 26b

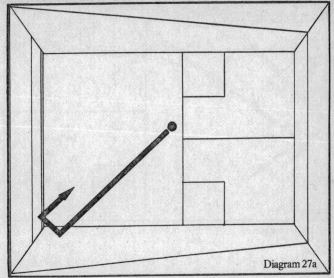

Reverse angle shot: hit towards far side wall.

Skid boast.

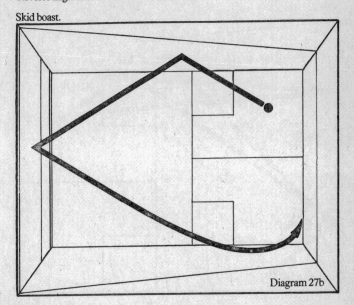

Diagram 27b

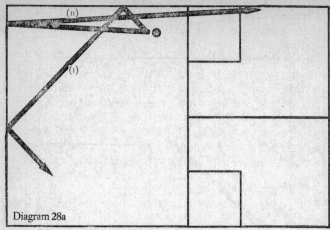

Diagram 28a

(i) Use of angle instead of (ii) drive from front of court.

(i) Use of angle instead of (ii) drive from back of court.

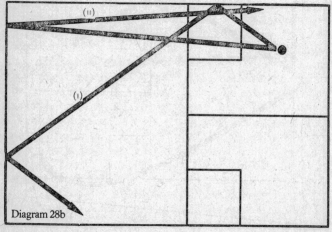

Diagram 28b

64

offensively or defensively, depending on where you are in the court, and can also be used to turn a defensive position into an attacking one.

In striking the ball, the technique is the same as for a drive with the weight on the front foot at the moment of impact, a good backswing, and ample follow-through. The ball needs pace as it has to contend with the deceleration which impact with the side wall will cause. There is only one way to learn how to get the angles right and what amount of lift you will need to carry the ball – and that is to go on the court and experiment until you are satisfied. Then practise what you have learned by trial and error until you can play the shot with regularity when you need it.

The angle shot can be played on either the forehand, the backhand, or even as a smash. It can be played from the front or the back of the court. It is particularly useful when your opponent is behind you as, if you shape up to it correctly, he can easily be deceived about the ball's direction. He may anticipate a drive down the wall, a drop shot, or even a lob. He may also anticipate an angle shot but if you hear him coming you can change it. For instance, if you are in the front of the court and he anticipates (in spite of your deceptive stance and backswing) that an angle shot is to be played against the forehand side wall, bringing the ball over across the court to the backhand side wall, and he moves in that direction, you can instantly change your plan and hit the ball early down the side wall leaving him stranded. See diagram 28a.

To hit a forehand angle shot is not technically different from the other shots, i.e. backswing, good balance, wrist cocked and racket up, weight on to the front foot and knees bent, racket face slightly open, eye on the ball maintaining the wrist cocked, and follow through after hitting the ball. The moment of impact will depend on the direction you wish the ball to follow and the extent of holding the racket face open will depend on how high you need or intend to hit the ball on to the side and front walls. If you hit the ball too early you will naturally end up with a cross-court shot, and if you hit it too late your ball may not reach the front wall. See diagram 29.

These angle shots are all straight angles – i.e. a straight angle shot is hit towards your nearside side wall. The reverse angle

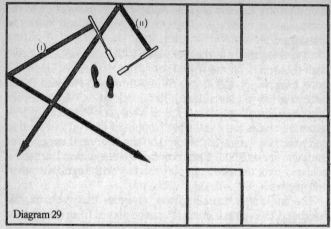

Diagram 29

Intended boast – errors: (i) the ball has been hit too early, hence a crosscourt shot (ii) too late, hence the ball hardly reaches the front wall.

Back wall boast: to be used only as a last resort, as it is difficult not to set up an opening for your opponent.

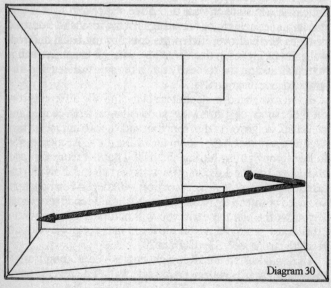

Diagram 30

shot is hit towards the far side wall. See diagram 27a. The reverse angle is useful as a deceptive shot – you can make the motions of playing a crosscourt drive, then instead of hitting the ball opposite the front foot you can hit it early so that it hits the far side wall first and moves along the front of the court, hitting the wall and landing back in your side. Your opponent,. if he has misread your shot and been duly deceived, will be left groping just behind and to the back of the T, to which position he had moved in anticipation of your drive.

These are some of the uses of the angled shot. Basically, use the angle as an offensive shot from the front of the court and a defensive shot from the back. Use the extra time these shots give you to regain position and balance.

We cannot proceed without a quick mention of the back wall boast. This is not a shot to be encouraged unless you are in severe difficulty, because it is so easy to set up an opening for your opponent. If the ball has passed you completely in the back of the court and will not be rebounding from the back wall as it is such a good length, you can turn to chase it and hit it upwards against the back wall with sufficient pace to carry it over to the front wall. The pace at which you strike the ball is not as important as the angle. Hit the ball in a direction as parallel as possible to the side wall; if it hits the side wall and has not been struck with sufficient pace, it may not reach the front wall. The best place to aim for the ball to hit the front wall is certainly in one of the corners. If it lands in the middle it will be an easy return for your opponent. Use this shot sparingly – when it is the only course of action.

5 ADVANCED TACTICS AND PRACTICE

Advanced Tactics

There are so many different ways in which a squash player can hit the ball and so many variations of each shot that inevitably there are limitless ways of playing a point or rally. One of the most exciting and enthralling experiences is to watch a match between two high-class squash players each looking for and trying to capitalise on the other's weakness. If there is no obvious weakness, the struggle becomes almost intellectual as the ball weaves a design about the court that makes full use of the space available.

If and when you have mastered the various stroke techniques and are able to hit the ball more or less in the right direction (i.e. the direction in which you are aiming) then the game becomes a battle of wits between you and your opponent, assuming that he is of a similar standard. The wits required will be tactical wits, and the outcome of the match will probably depend on the tactical ingenuity of one of the players. This presumes, of course, equal standard not only of stroke production, but also as far as fitness and stamina are concerned.

Basically, the art of tactics is placing the ball where your opponent will find it hardest to reach and making things as difficult as possible for him (strictly within the rules and a normal code of conduct).

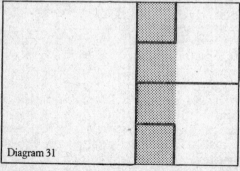

Diagram 31

Mistake area: the shaded part of the diagram shows the area where more than 50% of point-losing errors are made.

Your winning tactics should start before you go on court. This is not to encourage the use of strong-arm tactics in the changing room – 'the last chap I played here was taken off to hospital with blood oozing from more than one wound' type of thing. That is definitely nothing to do with squash tactics and is to be discouraged, apart from the fact that your opponent may decide to despatch you in similar fashion.

Tactics start with your equipment. You need clean white clothes, a properly strung racket, and shoes without broken laces. Then you must think of the background of the match, i.e. is it an individual or a team event. If it is a team event, which member of the opposing team will you be playing; have you played him before; who won – and why – and how; what are his strong points. What is his forehand like, and his backhand. If you have not played him yourself, possibly one of your team-mates has. The more you can discover about your opponent before you start, the better equipped you will be in your mind about how to deal with him. That is match preparation which must form part of your overall strategy.

When you arrive at a club for a match, especially if the club is unknown to you, check the courts – the height of the ceiling or roof – to see if you can use your lofted lobs. Is it a fast court (hot) or a slow court (cold)? These conditions may have an effect on the way you want to play the match.

Tactics have been mentioned all through this book, as an early guide as to how to start moving the ball around the court, and in connection with the individual strokes. This chapter is to try to help you string together the purpose of tactics as a whole, by relating the individual tactics which can be utilised for each stroke. In a way every stroke played is like a brick in a wall; when one brick is laid, you have to lay another until you get one layer which amounts to a point. The layers are added on until you have a wall nine layers deep – the nine points you need to win a game. When you have built three perfect walls, then you will have won the match.

The point of looking at it this way is to see the importance of each brick in the wall, or each stroke in the rally. Do not think of each shot as it comes along – think ahead and work out how best to manoeuvre your opponent into a losing position by building up a series of strokes that will move him up and down and across the court. His energy reserves will be used up, which can only benefit you in the long run. If you move him around enough, he will eventually make a slip and either hit a ball that you can play for a winner, or make a forced error himself. Each shot should be a tactical part of the whole strategy you are planning to win that point.

Concentration will be required to keep the plan going and also to notice any weakness in his game. You cannot afford to let your mind wander, and you do not have time to stand and watch your shots or your opponent's. You must keep the pressure on him all the time – try not to give him time to think or plan.

Any plan you do devise must, of course, be flexible. Your opponent will certainly have different ideas about you gaining the upper hand and will do his best to keep *you* under pressure. Thus, you cannot plan more than a few strokes ahead as he will probably try to put you off your plan by introducing a devious shot or two of his own into the fray. This may put a temporary spanner in the works, but you must not allow it to deter you from subtly returning to the original plan or devising a new one. While working out your strategy, don't allow yourself to neglect your opponent's strong points and the way in which he has played certain points or shots up until the moment in question. If he seldom missed the nick when given a high forehand shot along the side wall, then the chances are that he will not miss again and you should keep the ball away from that area.

When you start a match, use the knock-up to see if your opponent has any obvious, or even hidden, weaknesses. Also use it to accustom yourself to the court and the pace of the ball. From then on, do not stereotype your game – keep experimenting and changing so that your opponent does not become used to a particular pattern of play. Mix up your serves, giving him a majority of lob serves but throwing in a hard service or two for good measure. However, if he is finding your lob service easy to read and is coping with it too well for your liking, you should change it quickly and then come back to it later when it is to be hoped that he will be out of the habit of hitting winners off it. Change can be accomplished by altering the height, the pace, or even the direction of the service.

When the game is in progress, remember the principal points – try and dominate the T position and keep the ball away from your opponent, then bring your expertise with lob, drop shot, boast, and volley into play. Go for safe shots unless a winner seems certain and keep the pressure on your opponent. Play away from him and keep him behind you as much as possible.

The art of deception should also be used in sending your opponent in the wrong direction. The backswing, footwork, and timing are vital ingredients of any stroke, and taking these items a stage further you should learn how to deceive your opponent into thinking you are aiming for one shot and then playing another, i.e. shaping up for a forehand drive, then hitting the ball late and using a boast instead. Deception should be used to get an opponent moving in the wrong direction and to create openings.

Gamesmanship and Tactics

Gamesmanship can be considered to be a form of tactics in most games. It appears in squash as in other games – particularly in needle matches that mean a great deal to both winner and loser. Gamesmanship is not, perhaps, the most gentle form of tactics but it can be used to good effect – if you are in need of that sort of assistance. Personally I feel that there are two types, one of which may be used and the other which should be avoided.

The aim of gamesmanship at its most effective level is to disturb your opponent's concentration and, usually, to make him annoyed. Personally, I do not like its use in this form. An opponent who tries to annoy me or upset my concentration is not the sort of opponent I will play more than once, unless forced to do so.

It is fair enough to capitalise on an opponent's condition but this cannot really be termed gamesmanship. If an opponent is out of breath, and you don't wait for him to recover, that is still fair play. By all means, keep him under pressure like that.

Equally, it is fair to play upon an opponent's weakness, such as a poor backhand volley. But you must decide whether to concentrate your efforts on hitting the ball continuously towards his backhand (in which case it may improve) hoping he will send back a weak return; or whether you should only concentrate on his weak shot when you really need to put the pressure on and gain a point.

In the same 'fair' category must come the question of age. If your opponent is older than average for an active squash player, it stands to reason that although he may have years of guile and cunning that he can use to good effect on court, he is also less agile and his legs will not last as long as they used to. Move him around, make him stretch, bend, and run, for these are legitimate means of tiring your opponent and gaining the upper hand.

Gamesmanship is not cheating, although sometimes it is so close to it that the distinction is almost imperceptible. Remember one thing – very few, if any, champions have had recourse to the art of gamesmanship to help them win. They have been far too concerned with the vital aspects of their own progress to stoop to methods that might be considered dubious.

Practice
Squash has an immediately obvious advantage over nearly all other games because you can practise alone for as long as you wish. All you need is a court. It may not be so enjoyable to practise like this, but there is no doubt that it is the only way to really improve and perfect your strokes and your ability to vary their use to fit the occasion. The old maxim 'practice makes perfect' may be a bit corny but it still holds true. Practice can also provide you with plenty of exercise if you are sufficiently self-disciplined not to be lazy about it.

Most people practise too little and play too much, though others find practice as invigorating and enjoyable as playing. The main object of practice is to improve, but the exercise value will also do you good.

When practising, be sure that the strokes you are playing are the correct ones – it is just as easy to learn faulty technique on a stroke as good technique. Groove the shots rhythmically until they become automatic. We have looked at all the strokes in the book – now it is for you to practise them – first alone, and then with a partner.

Ball control must be high on the list of priorities for practice. Until you can control the ball, you will be lost. Irrespective of where you are and how the ball is hit to you, can you hit it in the manner and direction that you have chosen? You need good reflexes to move into the correct position to hit the ball at all,

Jonah Barrington, six times British Open Champion, perfectly balanced at the beginning of a backhand drive.

Geoff Hunt, British Open Champion and World No 1 in 1974, shows that eye on the ball is imperative as he prepares to unleash a powerful backhand volley from just behind the short line.

Gogi Alauddin is already moving from the T to cut off Qamar Zaman's drive down the wall. Zaman has hit the drive under severe pressure on the wrong foot, but his concentration keeps his eye on the ball as Gogi's long strides take him into a commanding position.

Gogi Alauddin, twice British Amateur Champion and World No 2 in 1974, keeps his wrist cocked and shortens his grip on the racket to retrieve a drive down the backhand wall; his knees are bent, enabling him to get right down to the ball. Ken Hiscoe is perfectly placed on the T, watching his every move.

Hiddy Jehan, World No 4 in 1974, shows the stance to adopt at the T position. His wrist is cocked, keeping the racket head up.

Ken Hiscoe, former British Amateur Champion and World No 2, shows how to get down to the ball even in the centre of the court as he concentrates fiercely on a backhand drop shot.

Sajjad Muneer, another top tenner in world squash, reaches up to achieve sufficient power and accuracy for a smash.

Heather McKay, World Champion for 13 years in 1974, has not lost a match for a decade. Here she has just hit a forehand drive down the wall; the weight of her body has been transferred to the front foot and her follow-through will finish just above her shoulder.

John Easter could be about to hit one of a number of shots. His knees are bent, getting him down to the ball as the backswing is at its peak. From this position he can decide to play a straight or crosscourt drive, a lob, a drop shot, a boast, or even a reverse angle.

apart from hitting it in the right direction. To do this well you must learn ball control by constant practice.

Learn to use the entire size of the court in terms of moving your opponent around; place the ball where he is not, or where he will find it hard to reach – either by a direct shot, or by a deceptive shot which will make him change direction. Ball control is needed for these manoeuvres – control before power or pace should be your maxim.

A lucky shot is something you cannot practise. Desperate lunges at the ball may result in occasional points, but do not rely on them to win matches for you. Don't bother to practise the blocked service return hit off the wood. If you do it in a match be thankful you were lucky enough to hit a return at all and practise the real thing afterwards.

Control, timing, flexibility in changing the shot after you have begun the backswing, change of pace – all these points should be practised in conjunction with the shots. Practice conditions should be similar to those for a match and your mental discipline must force you to work hard at it. Only if you have experienced real pain in terms of hard work in practice sessions can you hope to have the stamina and graft to outlast a tough opponent on court.

Each shot should be attempted from a new position with variations of pace and spin – and of course you must work at these shots from both the forehand and the backhand sides.

Several short practice sessions are thought to be better than a few long ones. It appears that between sessions, provided that they are frequent, the mental processes are able to absorb knowledge which increases the ability on court after the interval. In other words, after one session has finished the mind will continue to absorb knowledge from it, so that there may be a marked improvement in performance between one session and the next, as long as the interval is not too long.

Individual Practice
Practice on your own is obviously harder work but in the long term it will certainly be worth it. To begin with, use the practice sessions to groove your strokes and gain experience while also introducing the possibilities already mentioned, such as change of pace, spin, and height.

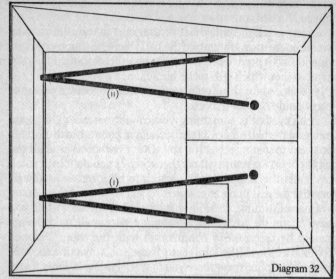

Diagram 32

Practising (i) forehand drives and (ii) backhand drives: stand just behind the service box and hit the ball up and down the side wall.

Ball control: stand at A and hit the ball so that it bounces between the dotted line and the short line, then try drives to the back of the court, i.e. into shaded area.

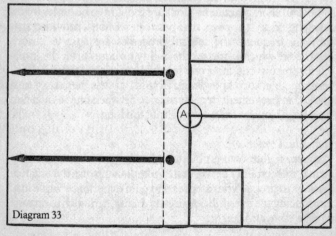

Diagram 33

74

The first stroke to practise is the drive. Place yourself in the forehand court just behind the service box and hit the ball up and down the side wall. Each shot should land in the service box. Practise until you get 10 out of 10 shots in the box. This will help you acquire the instinctive ability to hit the ball to a reasonable length.

Next, practise the same thing with the backhand drive. Don't worry too much about pace until you have found the length; then increase the pace. Divide the drive into sections - before, during, and after, and go through the technique for each section carefully, applying it studiously to the practice sessions. The drive into the service box cannot be practised too often.

As an additional ball control measure, move forward to the T and practise hitting the ball so that it lands about three feet from the front wall. Imagine a line parallel to the short line a yard up the court and hit the ball back to yourself somewhere between the imaginary line and the short line. This is merely useful for ball control as you are close enough to the front wall for a shot hit with pace to make you react fast to return the ball satisfactorily to the front. Your reflexes and ball control can be improved by gradually speeding up the process until you can carry out this exercise at a fast pace five or six times consecutively.

Then move your practice to the side walls at the back of the court. Stand about four feet in from the back wall and practise your drives up and down the side wall. Try to hit to a perfect length as much as possible and try to keep the ball up and down the side wall. When you begin to find it really difficult to return the ball, you are making good progress - for in other words you are beginning to beat yourself.

In practising the drive you can also practise hitting the ball from the same position early, at the top of the bounce, and late - but in the same direction, i.e. not using the early position to bring the ball round as in a crosscourt forehand. This will help you develop the use of the wrist in determining the direction of the shot.

Moving on from the drive, practice sessions should always include serving. The service is the only shot in the match for which you have time to prepare. It is probably less interesting practice, being less active than the other shots, but it is still most important.

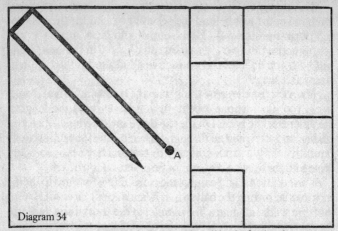

Diagram 34

Angles: stand at A and play the ball to the side wall by the forehand corner so that it returns to you. Repeat.

Drop shot: start 4ft from the front wall and work slowly back until you reach the T.

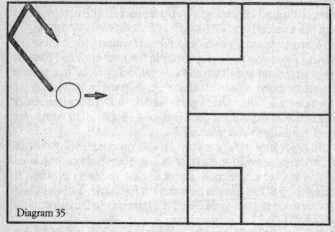

Diagram 35

Another form of practice is to hit the ball up against the front wall as often as you can – see how long you can keep going before the ball bounces twice or you hit the ball down or miss it. Also try to do this by not stepping in front of the short line and by confining the returns to the back quarters of the court.

Don't go on practising until you are bored. If you do, the benefit of the session may be lost. Only continue for as long as you find it enjoyable and interesting.

Individual practice can include angle shots, volleys, and drop shots. For angle shots you should position yourself to the left and slightly in front of the T. (As in diagram.) Play the ball to the side wall by the forehand corner and it should come back to you so that you can continue to practise the same stroke.

With volleys, stand about six feet from the front wall and hit the ball to and fro without letting it touch the floor. Gradually increase the distance from the front wall and try to keep the ball going in the air.

The drop shot can be practised quite far up in the front of the court. Start four feet away and work slowly backwards until you are practising from the T. All these variations will give you the ability to repeat the shots you need in a match, after much practice.

Practising in twos: A hits a boast from the back of the court, while B returns with a crosscourt drive to the side wall.

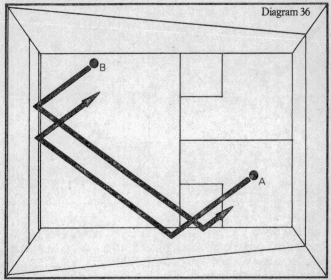

Diagram 36

Practice with Partner

Practising with a partner you can repeat many of the exercises which you set yourself as an individual. However, as those exercises are probably better practised on your own, use the time you have with a friend to do something more constructive.

The most useful form of practice in twos is to have one player in the front of the court on one side and one player at the back on the other. With this formation you can practise the lob, the boast, the drop, the volley, the crosscourt drive, and so on. As you have a partner you can keep pressing him as if he was an opponent, trying to beat him although each of you is only allowed to use one basic stroke. This creates the right atmosphere and will assist both of you to concentrate harder.

To repeat – the most important thing to practise in order to improve is hitting the ball to a good length. Unless you are able to do this, you are unlikely to go very far.

6 COURT BEHAVIOUR AND SAFETY

It is important to realise at an early stage that both you and your opponent are moving around at speed in a fairly confined area. Your opponent will often be very close to you and sometimes too close for safety, whether he is in front of you where you can see him, or behind you where you cannot. You must learn to limit your swing in such a way that the racket does not become a dangerous weapon.

You and your opponent must ensure that you give each other room to play and that you do not hinder each other's right to return the ball. Be particularly careful with the follow-through which has been known to cause severe injury. It is not necessary when you are at close quarters for your racket to continue its follow-through at the same pace after the ball has been struck. This should diminish in pace and you should attempt to keep your racket close to your body and under control. In spite of the small area in which squash is played, it is quite easy to play safely and still enjoy the game just as much. Don't allow your, or your opponent's, enjoyment of the game to deteriorate because of dangerous play.

You should always arrive a few minutes early for a match or even a friendly club game. This is not always possible, but you should always intend to leave a few minutes spare between arrival at the club and going on court to play. You may need to park the car, or your bus or train may be delayed. Too many club players tend to arrive at exactly the moment they are due on court. They have rushed to get there, have to pay the court fee before playing, and to change, and consequently arrive on court five minutes late. Not only is this bad manners to your opponent but you have also missed valuable court time. Quite apart from that, you will already be out of breath and flustered while your opponent will have his eye in and his mind on the game.

If you are playing in a match, you are allowed five minutes for a knock-up. Use the time to have a proper one, and accustom yourself to the feel of the court and the ball. Allow your opponent an equal number of balls to hit. There is nothing more annoying than having a knock-up with someone who never seems to send you any. Offer to change sides when your opponent feels he has had enough of one side.

When the time comes to open the match, if you are serving make sure that your opponent is ready to receive. Do not begin until you have looked over and seen that he is in position.

Once the match has started, the important thing is to keep out of your opponent's way. The correct tactical approach is to head for the T position at the first opportunity, but that is not much use if your opponent is already stationed there. Do be reasonable about your right to the T position. There is no reason why he should give it up if you have been unable to manoeuvre him away. Likewise, if you are dominating it, don't move if you can legitimately keep your opponent at bay.

If your opponent asks for a let, give it to him – it is better not to argue. You may feel that he doesn't deserve one, but if he is able to ask then he must feel that he does. If you feel he was wrong, try not to let him have any more by keeping out of his way. Also, if you hit your opponent with either racket or ball, apologise properly and offer him a let if the occasion justifies it or if you yourself would expect a let in similar circumstances.

Another important point to consider in terms of court manners is when you are obstructing your opponent, albeit by mistake, from taking a shot at the ball. Don't wait for him to ask for a let; give it to him automatically if you know it is your fault.

If you are in front of your opponent at any time and the ball is his to return, then if he hits you it is his point if the ball would have gone straight to the front wall. Therefore it is obviously better (and more comfortable) to keep out of the way.

If there is doubt about whether a ball was up or not, it is always better to play a let unless you have a marker who can make the decision for you. Never knowingly take a point for a ball that has bounced twice or that you have hit twice.

One last point. If you wear glasses and you are taking up squash, you may like to consider the advantages of contact lenses. It is perfectly possible to play squash wearing glasses but unless you are extremely careful they may slip and be broken. Also, if you happen to be playing a rather wild opponent, there is a chance that in his enthusiasm his racket may dislodge your glasses and possibly cause injury. Not only may you feel less vulnerable wearing contact lenses, but some people claim that vision is improved more with them than glasses.

7 FITNESS AND TRAINING

Fitness

Squash requires a good eye, a strong wrist, great activity, and considerable judgement for success. However, the most important thing in squash today is fitness in terms of stamina, strength, and speed. Of all modern popular sports, squash has the highest rate of energy expenditure.

Fitness for squash consists of increasing the efficiency of the heart, the muscle cells, the circulatory system, the lungs, and so on. As far as the heart is concerned, fitness will require an increase in the heart muscles' size; with muscle cells, the volume of muscle must increase; with circulation, the blood will need to move faster in greater quantities to the right areas; the lungs will need increased capacity, and the body will need to be rid of excess fat. All these organic improvements can be achieved by taking regular hard exercise which will result in an all-round improvement of body efficiency, including more stable heat dispersion. Heat loss can be a problem if you are unfit, resulting in a too-fast rise in temperature, which can be dangerous. If you are fit, heat dispersion is more regulated, taking a more even course.

Fitness also means that agility, coordination, reflexes, and balance are all at their peak. The degree of physical fitness depends on general health and nutrition. One cannot be physically fit without a balanced diet of proteins, fats, carbohydrates, minerals, and vitamins. In other words, eat plenty of meat, fish, eggs, fresh vegetables, salads, cheese etc.

Moderation in both food and drink is recommended. Alcohol should not be consumed in large quantities – it is genuinely harmful to the system, however enjoyable it may be at the time. There is certainly nothing wrong or harmful about the consumption of wine or beer, but not before playing. In fact, if you are competing in a match it is suggested that you decline offers of anything alcoholic for the previous 24 hours or so.

Never play on a full stomach. Be sensible about what you eat within a few hours of playing. There are, of course, exceptions to the rule, but by and large you will find it more comfortable not to eat anything heavy two or three hours before playing.

Smoking has been proved to be positively harmful to health generally. It is also particularly bad for the sportsman who needs all the capacity his lungs can give him and therefore it is generally discouraged.

Fitness refers principally to stamina; the best way to increase yours is by running, which is covered in the training section of this chapter.

Speed is another element of fitness. Without it you cannot hope to return to the T fast enough, or to reach the ball if it is hit away from you. Anticipation and quick thinking can save you some energy but unless you are playing somebody who cannot take advantage of your sluggishness (in which case you are very lucky) you will need to develop speed. This is covered in the next section as far as circuit training is concerned. However, there is a test you can do with a friend to develop both your speed and general fitness. Take a box of old squash balls on court (12 balls) and empty them out all over the court. Then time yourself running round and picking them up. Then let your friend do it. Do this two or three times, each time trying to do it faster. When you start again next day or a few days later, try and beat the previous fastest time. This exercise need not, of course, be done on the court.

If you have not played squash before or if you have not taken any exercise for a long time, start gently. Hit the ball around for 15 minutes or so on the first day and gradually build up. It can be disastrous to take violent exercise all at once when you are not used to it. Your heart may not like the sudden extra work it is being made to do, or you may pull a muscle you did not know you had.

Sleep
The amount of sleep required by an individual will vary depending on occupation, age, and possibly sex, although it is not clearly established that men require more sleep than women. Some people require at least eight hours sleep a night while others are able to survive on far less. Some people, too, are able to restore themselves with short naps of a few minutes at a time. If you are used to a certain pattern of sleep then it will be hard to break it – you will find it tiring to change until a new pattern becomes a habit.

Once again, we encounter variations that depend on an individual's way of life or metabolism. If your job entails using your mind, it is generally thought that you will require more sleep than a manual worker. Young people certainly need more sleep than old; in fact, it can be said that as you grow older you require less and less sleep, although the average requirement for an adult is estimated at about eight hours per night – thus one third of your life should be spent asleep in order for you to get the most out of the remaining two thirds.

Occasional lack of sleep will not have any detrimental effect but regular loss will result in tiredness and lack of concentration. You may also become short-tempered. However, it is unlikely that permanent damage will arise from consistent lack of sleep and the ill-effects it causes, as nature usually intervenes well before such a stage is reached. One really good night's sleep can help you 'catch up' on a considerable deficit.

Sex

A great deal has been written about the effect of sexual intercourse on the sportsman. However, I do not propose to go into detail in this book on the subject of sex and sport. There is nothing to suggest that sex will have a detrimental effect on your squash-playing provided that you have allowed sufficient time after sex for the body to readjust itself. A good night's sleep after sex will be perfectly sufficient to allow your body the readjustment period it needs as well as sufficient sleep in normal circumstances.

Naturally, there are exceptions to this rule. Apparently, at least one world record has been broken by an Olympic champion within an hour of making love. If you wish to experiment on your own individual possibilities, it is recommended that you do not do so when you have a particularly hard match on court to follow.

Travel Fatigue

A short note on jet lag may be appropriate to the transatlantic or long-distance traveller who also plays squash.

The body has its own time clock that works on a 24-hour cycle, tuned to familiar rhythms at home. When the pattern of living changes by being transported to another continent, the body system is thrown upside down as it tries to live life to the old system while you are imposing a new system and clock. Adjustments to new environments and timings can take up to about a week.

There is no cure for this. However, it is best to try and attune the body slowly to the new system, avoiding an abrupt change. Don't try to play squash within 24 hours of arriving. It may be physically possible, but it may not be sensible.

Training

Circuit training is a succession of carefully selected and related exercises which are repeated. By courtesy of the BP International Tennis Fellowship, we include here an excellent training programme designed to raise the level of general health and fitness.

Training Programme

This is designed to raise your level of *general* fitness in terms of speed, strength, and stamina. Each week there are three days of running plus exercises, three of exercises only, and one day of rest.

RUNNING

Running is basic to any form of fitness because it improves the efficiency of the body's heart/lung and heart/circulation mechanisms. There are three types of running:

Middle distance (1–4 miles). Do this at a fast stride and time each run. Push yourself or it will do you no good.

Intervals. Run for the stated time at a fast stride. Rest for the same length of time. Repeat. Don't flag over the last few.

Sprints. Mark out a distance of 25 yards. Jog up to the starting point and cover this distance flat out.

THE EXERCISES

Press-ups. Front support position on toes and palms with hands a shoulder width apart and body straight. Bend arms. Straighten arms. Repeat.

Sit-ups. Lie flat on your back and clasp hands behind neck. Sit up and press forehead towards knees keeping legs straight. Repeat.

Swallows. Lie flat on tummy and clasp hands behind back. Keep legs and arms straight as you push hands down back of legs while raising head, shoulders, and chest off ground. Repeat.

Burpees. Front support position (as for press-ups). Keep palms on floor and jump legs forward so that toes are between hands. Jump legs back again. Repeat.

Bench steps. Find a bench or seat that you can step on to only with difficulty. Step up and down on bench getting both legs straight while on it. Lead with left foot first going up and down. Change to lead with right foot after doing half number of repetitions.

Double Knee Jumps. Stand lightly on tiptoe. Leap high off the ground while bouncing knees against chest. Repeat as a continuous rebounding movement without a skip in between.

Pull-ups. Overgrasp on a beam. Without pushing off with your feet pull yourself up until your chin is level with beam. Lower. Repeat.

Skipping. Get yourself a good heavy rope and vary the steps but always aim to land as lightly as possible. Try to work non-stop for the stated time.

NB It is important to go through the full range of movement each time at each exercise.

THE TEST RATE AND THE TRAINING RATE

We all have different builds and different strengths so the number of repetitions you do at each exercise will depend on your individual capacity.

Before starting on the programme establish your own test rate. Do as many repetitions as you can at each of the exercises in one minute – or until you can do no more, whichever is sooner. This is your test rate. Your training rate is half the test rate (round off odd numbers upwards).

A CIRCUIT

Do each exercise once at the training rate. This is one circuit. Repeat and be sure to do the exercises in the same order as before.

General

1 Before you start any form of training – running or exercises – *always* warm up with five minutes' jogging in warm clothing.

2 Remember training is not an end in itself. It is designed to help you to play better squash and is never a substitute for practice. However, fitness is something that no opponent can deprive you of and in these days of increasing competition only the fittest will survive.

In addition to the training programme above, carefully supervised weight training can be very beneficial to general strength in important areas – legs, shoulders, stomach, wrists, etc. Another excellent way to strengthen the wrist and build up the muscles is to have a squash ball in the pocket and squeeze it constantly.

Obviously, more sophisticated training procedures are available, but commonsense variations of what has been mentioned above are considered to be quite adequate.

There are some people who claim that the best method of training for squash is to play it. There is certainly an element of truth in that – but it may not be the most effective in the long run.

8 MATCH PLAY AND CHAMPIONSHIP SQUASH

Once the technique of hitting the strokes correctly has been mastered, squash reverts to being a game, in common with many others, of strategic wit and stamina. Provided that the physical strength is also there, with concentration you will win points. Squash is a fast game, and the need for tactical expertise will be forced upon you by any opponent of a reasonable standard. In order to bring all your tactical experience to bear upon a match, you will need to concentrate hard, not allowing your mind to wander.

Concentration and determination are complementary, and one will be wasted if the other is missing in a player. That would be a gap in any player's match-playing ability as it is these two characteristics that help a champion on his way to the top.

When you are playing in a match, do not let your eyes or mind wander from the court. Keep your eyes focused on the ball (or your feet if the ball is not in play), and try to ignore interruptions.

There are many factors that help a squash player to become a champion. Real pleasure in actually playing squash must be a contributory factor. Few, if any, champions at any sport reach the top level without enjoying what they are doing. The effect of success makes it even more enjoyable, just as constant failure can have the opposite effect.

To reach the top, few players can afford not to be perfect in terms of technical and tactical expertise. Beginners have everything to learn and advancement will only come if the tuition is good. The basic strokes must be grasped before additional more sophisticated techniques are learnt. Tactics then begin to play a role, and gradually a player's thinking must concentrate more on tactics than on stroke production. Stroke production should be nearly automatic. A champion develops when all these points are second nature to him and this can only come from years of hard slog and practice.

Practice probably consumes most of the time required for improvement. Consistent improvement comes if every practice shot is executed with controlled physical effort and applied thought. You must be completely dedicated and involved.

Attention to detail also plays a vital part. A champion will not only check that all his equipment is perfect – that the tension of his racket stringing is correct and that his racket handle has a fresh, comfortable grip – but will also pay attention to minute detail of strokes and tactics. Attention to detail in the quality and quantity of diet also plays a part for champions.

The will to win and determination and drive that go with it make up an important part of the psychological armoury of the complete player. The 'killer instinct' as it is known is important in key matches when the outcome of one point may change the course of a match. Nerves at the moment of truth can ruin an otherwise brilliant player's career.

So now you are ready to play a match. Obviously there are many points to remember which have been mentioned during the course of the book and which we will not repeat now. But do remember to run after every ball – if you don't, how can you hope to win the point? However you scramble it back, your opponent may miss it – always remember there is a chance.

Playing matches is a natural sequel to learning the game. Any sport, apart from the exercise value, is supposed to instil competitiveness in you, which is what match play does.

Squash reflects the true personality of a player, because everything happens so fast that he has to revert to his natural self. If you are casual, it will show in your playing, and similarly if you are determined or aggressive.

Matches are the proving ground of all your endeavours on the squash court, and this chapter is to help you fulfil your ambitions to win matches. If you know that you are playing a match at a certain time on a certain day, take care not to have a large meal on that day until after the match. Have a light lunch and consume enough fuel to keep your engines running at full pitch for the match. Ensure that whatever food you eat on the day is full of protein and nourishment. If you have had a steak the evening before, then that will be beneficial to your dietary fitness for the match. Also ensure that you get your full quota of sleep the night before a match – too little sleep, however fit you are, may begin to tell towards the end of a long match.

The subject of clothing has been covered in the early part of the book. If you feel brighter and happier when you are dressed in smart and trendy clothes, why not bring that feeling on to the court as well? Wear clean shirts and shorts, for apart from feeling sharper you will be a credit to your club if you dress smartly – and remember that the clothing should be white.

One top-class player who abhors the use of anything other than a completely clean outfit every time he plays is Gogi Alauddin of Pakistan. If an opponent dares to be so rude as to turn up in dirty clothes, Gogi will be furious and all the more encouraged to wipe him off the court. It should be noted that Gogi is a very gentle and unassuming character.

Attention to detail as far as your racket is concerned has also been mentioned. It may be that you are the proud owner of more than one racket, in which case take it with you and ensure it is in as equally good condition as the other. It would be unfortunate if your racket broke and you had to resort to another which was uncomfortable to hold and had poor tension in the frame. It might cost you several points before you became used to the change.

Do not forget your pre-match tactics. Study your future opponent if you get a chance before playing. Do not watch the ball but watch him – and closely. When his pattern of play emerges you can then plot and plan your tactics against him. If you have not had a chance to watch him, when you go on court you must watch the knock-up and the early stages of the match to find out how he plays. Keep an open mind on your opponent at all times. Don't plot too studiously as equally he may have watched you and devised a special pattern of play for the match – it may be quite different from the pattern you have seen. Points to look for are whether he tightens up or becomes nervous on certain points; whether he is a good volleyer; if he can cut off the ball in mid-court; if he presses home his advantages when in a winning position; whether he falters overhead, how tough he is when losing – whether he fights back desperately; what his weaknesses are, and so on. These are some of the questions to which you must know the answers. Once armed with this knowledge you can plan a bit further ahead.

In preparing yourself for the match, you must impress upon yourself the importance of *efficiency* on court. The only way to be as efficient as you possibly can is to reduce your margin of error to a minimum. Play a simple basic game – do not aim *one* nick above the tin if you do not *always* hit it above the tin. Aim one foot above for safety to reduce the margin of error. Play all the shots at your disposal safely and try to keep them in the four corners of the court. Efficient play is a stable foundation on which to base your game.

Always try to win by playing your own game and imposing it on your opponent, irrespective of your style of play, be it aggressive, dependent on accuracy, or consistency. The chances of winning a match when you have adapted to the style of your opponent may be limited. Always play within your capabilities and do not foolishly try to do more than you are able.

Play against your opponent's game, not his name or reputation. A determined effort against one who enjoys a better reputation than you is more likely to unsettle him. He has everything to lose and a reputation to protect, while you have everything to gain. This is one of the principal reasons established players lose to those who are less well-known; a good effort shakes them and allows an element of doubt to creep into their minds, causing uncertainty in their play.

Successful match-play depends upon finding your strengths and knowing your weaknesses and making the best of your knowledge. If you find you are losing, try to indulge in a little self-recrimination and decide the reasons. If your tactics are wrong, try to change them. If it is simply because your opponent's shots make it impossible for you to carry out the right tactics, then try to appreciate the fact that you will have to improve – there is always room for improvement.

Perhaps a little more pace on your shots, giving your opponent less time, will unbalance him and disturb his rhythm. You can achieve this either by hitting the ball earlier or by hitting it harder. Experience will show you what to do although the basic principle remains the same.

If you are winning, then keep on with the same tactics and perseverance. It is surprising how many apparently 'won' matches are lost by indiscreet changing of winning tactics.

Assuming that you have practised your shots, that they are working well, and that you are fit, then concentration may be the one single factor that separates a good player from a bad one. Concentration varies among individuals and you must work to improve yours if it is something you find difficult.

Never let your concentration slip in any circumstances. It can pull you out of the most depressing circumstances.

Remember that your opponent is human too and that he has feelings and reactions the same as yours. If you are in a tight position, don't forget that he may be suffering in the same way. Tension and physical exhaustion can affect him just as much as you. Don't isolate yourself from your opponent – keep fighting in case he is the first to crack.

You are there to win – so don't go out there to be a good loser.

9 MARKING AND REFEREEING

The incredible growth of interest in squash in this country has resulted in many more individuals playing the game at an ever increasing number of clubs. Both individuals and clubs have become interested in competitions, tournaments, and leagues.

All serious competitive squash matches should be controlled by a marker and a referee. A marker quite often handles the game almost completely, and in fact if there is a shortage of officials at a particular event, he may double as referee. The marker calls the score and makes the decisions while the referee, if there is one present, may be needed to adjudicate an appeal from one of the players on a decision made by the marker. Interpretation of the rules is also a referee's job, and the principal reason for his attendance.

The referee may interrupt a match if he thinks that the marker has made a mistake, or if he feels that a player has infringed the rule on fair view of the ball and freedom of stroke. If the referee thinks a player has not made sufficient effort to get out of the way of his opponent, then he can award a point to that opponent. If a player does not allow his opponent to have a fair view of the ball, i.e. if the ball is shielded by a player after it has hit the front wall in such a way as to prevent his opponent from seeing it quickly enough to make a stroke at it; or if he crowds his opponent by standing too close without actually obstructing; or if he prevents the opponent from having the whole front area of the court to aim for, then the referee should allow a let. However, if the referee thinks the player has done one of these three things deliberately rather than negligently, then he should award a penalty point to his opponent.

There is one more instance in which the referee can make a ruling. If a player is prevented by his opponent from making a winning shot, then the referee should award him a point. It will depend on the referee's experience how he estimates whether a winner could be produced from certain situations; for this reason, it is more or less essential that anyone who marks or referees a squash match also plays or has played the game to a reasonable standard; at least to a standard so that he understands the sort of situations with which he could be faced in making a decision.

These points are covered fully in the rules of the game at the end of this book. Obviously, if you are marking and-or refereeing a match, you must first have a clear working knowledge of the rules. Marking and refereeing are both important jobs in squash and not without interest. If you are an enthusiast, neither is a difficult task. A working knowledge of the rules is easy to acquire, because if you play, you will already know a good many of them. The Squash Rackets Association organises courses all over the country which are well worth attending if only to learn a bit more about the game.

It will take some time to acquire sufficient knowledge and confidence to mark top-class squash, but small beginnings often lead to other things – and there is a need for markers and referees to assist at competitive events at all levels. Confidence is needed because you will be required to make quick decisions, instinctively showing that you know what is right or wrong. If you have no confidence in your judgment, your players will certainly have none.

There are many refinements that a marker or referee will need to learn, but it must suffice to simplify the let and penalty situation. If a player is intentionally obstructed he is awarded a point; if it is accidental but he could have hit a winner, he is awarded a point; if it is accidental but the ball could have been returned then a let should be played.

Most of the points a prospective marker or referee needs to know are in the rules. It is not the intention of this book to go into greater detail on the subject. However, a marker should obviously apply common sense to the rules and when he has learnt all the correct calls he can begin to apply his knowledge.

One thing must be remembered. Very rarely have I heard a marker from the back of the gallery state the score sufficiently loudly for all the spectators as well as the players to hear. Quite often only the odd half dozen people close to the marker, apart from the players, can hear it. Everyone there will want to know, so speak loudly and clearly.

As far as scoring is concerned, a squash match consists of the best of five games, with each game being won by the first player to win nine points (provided that he is at least 2 points ahead). If

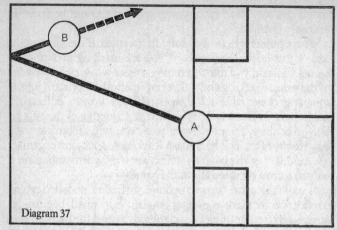

Diagram 37

If the ball hits B before he can return A's shot, then B loses the point.

If B (intentionally or not) prevents A's shot from hitting the front wall directly, A wins the stroke.

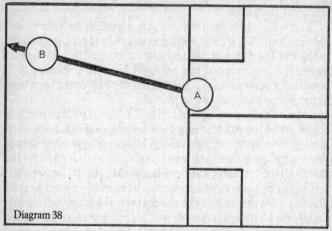

Diagram 38

the score reaches eight-all, the receiver can decide whether to play *set two* or *no set*. *Set two* means the first player to win the next two points and *no set* means the first player to win the next point – in either case the first player to win the points or point takes the game. In the case of *set two*, the points do not have to

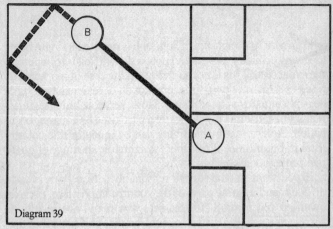

Diagram 39

If B (intentionally or not) prevents A's shot from hitting the front wall indirectly, then a let is played.

If A's shot hits B, but the ball would not have reached the front wall anyway, then A loses the stroke.

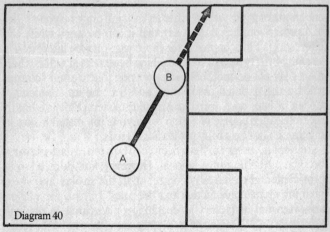

Diagram 40

be scored consecutively – your opponent may score a point between your two points.

The game does not go beyond 10 points. In the case of *set two*, the score can be 10-9 or 10-8 in favour of one player, and in the case of *no set* the score will be 9-8 to the winner.

10 COACHING

The growth in popularity of squash has resulted in there being too many ordinary players and not enough officials to cope with the expansion. This is not so serious in the case of markers and referees which are part-time jobs, for an occasional evening or possibly a match at a local club. However, coaching is a different matter, for this is not ideally a part-time or amateur occupation. A very reasonable living can be made in this country from it, but in spite of this there is a terrible shortage of qualified professional coaches.

If you want to take squash reasonably seriously, it is often difficult, and in some parts of the country impossible, to find a qualified coach at all. In this case you may have to rely on friends to teach you the basic requirements and hope that they are technically correct. Unfortunately, it is as easy to become familiar and well-grooved in strokes that are incorrectly produced as it is in the right ones.

Having said that coaching can provide a reasonable living, one should add that it is neither an easy job nor everyone's idea of a profession. Let us just say that it can be worthwhile and interesting. This chapter is for those who may be interested in learning briefly how to start coaching beginners at a club where there may not be another coach. It is possible to attend courses run by the national association and become an Elementary Coach or later an Approved Amateur Coach. This is a highly recommended course of action for anyone interested in coaching though not on a fully professional basis.

It is not necessary to have been or to be a top squash player to become a teaching professional. However, you do need to be proficient and technically correct at all the strokes and at explaining elementary tactics and the rules. In fact, top players are often unsatisfactory at coaching or teaching individuals who have only just started to play because they have forgotten what that stage was like in their own careers, and cannot bridge the gap to an understanding of the pupil's problems.

One notable exception to that rule is Jack Giles, the professional at the RAC, who retired undefeated after being Professional Champion of the United Kingdom for 10 years. When the Lambton Club opened he kindly came and coached some beginners. I was enormously impressed by his communication with his pupils and immediate diagnosis of their problems.

I was equally impressed when in a spare moment I saw him standing alone on the court near the T, hitting the ball to both sides of the front wall in such a way that the ball always returned to him in almost exactly the same spot. He hardly needed to move to keep the ball going – that is ball control.

Thus, communication with the pupil is of vital importance – the ability to get across to him what you want him to learn. Since every pupil is different, the coach must be able to get on easily with all types of people.

When taking a beginner on the court for the first time, you should first introduce him to the various parts of the court. It is not necessary to go into great detail about all the lines and boundaries at this stage but a quick mention of the front wall, the tin, the short line, and the boundary lines should be sufficient to keep him playing in the right direction.

You have probably already helped him choose a suitable racket – not only suitable for a beginner, but also taking into account his economic situation. You should start with a fast ball, as a yellow dot ball will almost certainly be much too dead for him to use. Before actually starting to hit it, you should of course show him the correct grip. Explain why that particular grip is the one to use and why it is successful.

Then place the pupil in the forehand court approximately on the short line and hit the ball to him off the front wall, suggesting that he returns it in a similar way. You may find you have a pupil who has played tennis, badminton, or cricket already, and who knows a bit about ball games and coordination of movement. So much the better. Alternatively, you may find you have somebody who initially seems quite uncoordinated, and who does not respond in the same way at all. In the latter's case, it is a question of perseverance; you must be patient and keep sending him the ball until he finally clicks. In this sort of situation, you must obviously help as much as you can and try to correct his mistakes – he may not have his eye on the ball or he may be aiming for a ball that bounces higher than the one you are using. Whatever he is finding difficult, you are there to help him.

It is always easier to teach beginners individually so that you can focus your full attention on that one pupil. It may be that you can teach three or four beginners at once if there is a shortage of time or courts, but be careful that you teach them all safety in the court and court manners just as well as you would an individual pupil. Court behaviour is important and should be discussed at an early stage, while safety *must* be discussed at the beginning of the first lesson as soon as your pupil has swung a racket for the first time. Accustom him to the fact that the racket can be used dangerously and cause injury right at the beginning of his squash career, and he will remember it.

Pupils of any age, particularly younger ones, have a limited learning capacity in a concentrated period. Generally, half-hour periods of continuous coaching are quite sufficient. In fact even better would be two periods of 15 minutes each, with a 15-minute gap in between. The increased learning capacity that this introduces is remarkable. However, that is usually impractical.

Concentrated coaching does not mean half an hour of solid talking about how to play. You should divide your time carefully into sections so that a few minutes talking is followed by an equal period of action on the court. If all the instruction is theoretical rather than practical, the pupil will become bored and his mind will wander, defeating the purpose of the lesson. So talk for a short while, then demonstrate, then let the pupil try. Most people learn faster by seeing and doing rather than reading or listening – this applies particularly to squash.

After the elementary start, the first stroke should obviously be the forehand. It should be followed by the backhand and then the other shots in a reasonable order, e.g. service, return of service, lobs, volleys, drop shots, and angles. In teaching all of these strokes be sure to point out the basic footwork necessary, the back swing (safely), the hitting of the ball (correct moment of impact), and the follow-through.

It is important to keep the pupil feeling that he is enjoying learning the game and that he is improving all the time. Don't let him feel uncomfortable at any time – even right at the beginning you must make him feel welcome, that you are personally interested in his progress, and that he has nothing to be self-conscious about. This is all part of the job of communication; the pupil will learn best in a happy and enthusiastic atmosphere.

It may be of interest to some readers that some excellent squash coaching films are now available for hire from the Squash Rackets Association, 70 Brompton Road, London, SW3 1DX. These are recommended to both coach and pupil.

Part Two

11 THE STATE OF THE GAME IN 1974

It is estimated that in 1963 there were fewer than 100,000 squash players in the United Kingdom. There are now somewhere between a million and a million and a half players, and the number is still increasing at the rate of approximately 50,000 players a year. This may not be the same staggering growth rate achieved over the past 10 years, but it is still remarkable.

In a decade when leisure has suddenly become an important business throughout the world, tennis has become a dynamic growth sport in most countries except for the United Kingdom and Australia. In these two countries the number of tennis players has remained fairly static while squash has boomed beyond all recognition, becoming the fastest-growing participatory sport, particular in England.

The rate of increase in the United Kingdom has been due to several factors. New public awareness of leisure coupled with a greater desire for fitness has resulted in people taking more exercise. Squash, being one of the most enjoyable methods of escaping from the choking urban rat-race and working off frustrations, was one of the principal activities to benefit. Squash is particularly suitable as a means of physical exercise for executives and those in the professions, and others whose time is important. A game of squash does not take too long and is therefore more preferable to the busy man in terms of time than a game of golf, cricket, or tennis. An added advantage is the fact that squash does not depend on the weather, being an indoor all-the-year-round sport.

In addition, the emergence of a British world champion, Jonah Barrington, captured the imagination of many people. Barrington's attractive personality and particular enthusiasm for the game, and his personal training methods, made him an object of admiration as well as heaping previously unknown publicity on the game.

Largely due to commercial squash-club developers and

promoters, squash began to boom, and the new clubs were quickly fully patronised. Commercial concerns found squash an attractive investment because of the substantial income to be obtained from subscriptions and court fees. With rising property costs, the comparatively small land area required for a successful squash club make such a venture a financially profitable concern.

With more and more courts becoming available (according to some sources, between three and four hundred more courts are built each year in the United Kingdom), there has always been the hope that facilities would go some way towards catching up with demand. Unfortunately with more and more people taking up the game, it is unlikely that this will be realised in the near future. The commercialisation of squash has undoubtedly led to an increase in the number of members per court at many clubs. With an estimated minimum of one million players in the United Kingdom playing on an estimated 2,500 courts in 1974, the average number of players per court is 400 – three times the recommended level. This merely serves to confirm the fact that demand still overwhelmingly exceeds capacity, in spite of new courts and facilities. Even if the number of participants remains the same as it is now (which is very unlikely), at least twice as many courts will still be required, so that one can confidently predict the continuation of the squash boom until at least 1980.

Meanwhile, the interest shown in this country has spread to Europe. Squash has been played in the United States, Canada, Australia, New Zealand, South Africa, India, and Pakistan since before the war, and it has since been taken up by many other countries all round the world. However, several European countries, whose interests have previously been directed towards tennis, have only recently become aware of the potential of squash. Sweden was the first such country to promote the game, and a minor boom resulted. Other countries are following suit. Spain, France, Germany, and Italy are yet to experience the pleasures of squash, but both Madrid and Paris will have their own squash facilities during 1974. Paris has two concrete courts, housed inside an unused real tennis court, which have been fully utilised by a limited number of players for many years; but an English company has recently opened a modern six-court centre in central Paris, and a four-court complex as part of the Internacional Club de Tennis, Madrid, has been opened there. Other clubs in other countries are bound to follow.

In the United States and Canada, a slightly different version of the game is played with a narrower court, a hard ball, and a more sturdy racket. In all other countries squash is played according to international (British) standard dimensions regarding size and specification of court, ball, and racket.

There have been several attempts to find common ground between these two different versions of the game. So far efforts to bring the two together have failed – thus international competition is not seriously practicable.

The basic theories governing the two games are similar. However, the international court is $2\frac{1}{2}$ feet wider at 21 feet, the length remains the same at 32 feet, and the board (tin) is 2 inches higher at 19 inches. Scoring is also different but the principal difference between the two games is the ball. The international ball is smaller, lighter, squashier, and much slower than the heavier, more solid American ball. The racket is only different so that it can cope with the heavier ball.

There is an interesting theory behind the differences in court size which is almost certainly true. In 1922, British officials decided to try and standardise the dimensions of a court. Up until that time courts had been built, both in the UK and in the USA, in a bewildering variety of sizes, largely dictated by the amount of space available. An average was taken of all the lengths and widths of existing courts and the result became the official international dimensions – 32 feet long by 21 feet wide. The same exercise was carried out in the United States two years later, but unfortunately American officials came up with a different answer. The length was the same but the width was only $18\frac{1}{2}$ feet. This difference has really remained one of the stumbling blocks of a compromise between the two games. It is easy enough to change the type of ball or racket in use, but to alter the size of the court is a very major and highly expensive manoeuvre.

In January 1974 a constructive effort towards finding common ground between the two games was made by the Lambton Squash Club in London. An invitation tournament, featuring eight of the world's finest players and involving a 'round robin' format of play, combined the use of American scoring with the otherwise international game. The result was less conclusive than it might have been, but it was proved that the different scoring methods do not contribute to otherwise insurmountable problems. The basic difference in the scoring methods is that in the international game a player may only score a point if he is serving; in the American version, the player who wins a rally scores a point whether he is serving or not and the first player to score 15 points rather than 9 wins a game.

It was also announced early in 1974 that negotiations were taking place to establish a world circuit of tournaments for the top players. This would be run on similar lines to the tennis circuits of the World Championship of Tennis and the Commercial Union Grand Prix. Obviously it is an ambitious plan but its success will be assured provided that sponsors can be persuaded to invest sufficient sums of money in the game.

If squash is to become as popular as it deserves not just amongst those who actually play, then another element must be added – the spectator. Developments over the past few years have shown that spectators will certainly go and watch good competitive squash if there is space for them to either sit or stand with a decent view of the court. Glass back walls have made viewing conditions simpler at many clubs and there are few major tournaments in the UK that do not make use of the technical advantages of a glass back wall, thereby vastly increasing spectator capacity. However, maximum capacity at most tournaments rarely exceeds two or three hundred.

Officials hope that television coverage of the game, undertaken for the first time in 1974, will result in more interest in watching rather than playing the game. However, the difficulties in really good television presentation have not yet been overcome and, therefore, if squash is to grow as a spectator sport, facilities for watching it live must be vastly increased. The future may lie in courts with four transparent plastic walls and seating capacity for several thousand spectators.

Squash is really still in the early stages of a potentially enormous boom. It is up to developers, promoters, and officials to ensure that the game's growth is directed along the right lines.

12 A BRIEF HISTORY

The game of squash rackets is generally thought to have had its
origin at Harrow School about 150 years ago when boys waiting for their turn to play rackets knocked a soft ball against
some walls outside the court.

Squash rackets is really the younger brother of the game
rackets, which was first recorded as being played at Harrow in
1820. The dimensions of a rackets court are considerably
greater than those of an international standard squash court –
the basic overall area is 60 feet by 30 feet, with the back wall 15
feet high and front and side walls about 30 feet high. A modern
squash court is 32 feet deep by 21 feet wide with back wall 7 feet
high and front wall 15 feet high.

Rackets is played with a hard ball, whereas squash uses a soft
ball, with which the name of the game is associated. Originally
neither rackets nor squash, with their general similarities, came
under the jurisdiction of a ruling body, but in 1907 the Tennis
and Rackets Association was formed to administer the games of
real tennis, rackets, and squash. It was not until 1929 that the
Squash Rackets Association was formed; this body now vir-
tually controls the game.

Whereas real tennis and rackets have remained fairly static in
terms of popularity and players, due mainly to shortage of
courts – the subsequent higher cost confining these two fine
games largely to the older universities and public schools –
squash began to develop from the 1930s. Before that time, there
was no definitive court size. As late as 1934 it was written in the
Encyclopedia of Sports, Games and Pastimes that 'the authorities
regard a court 42 feet long and 24 feet wide as excellent'. There
is no doubt that if a squash court was still to be built to these
dimensions the game would not have prospered as much as it
has in recent years. However, the dimensions of an international standard squash court were originally laid down by the
Tennis and Rackets Association in 1922; these dimensions
were confirmed as official when the SRA was formed seven
years later.

It is possible to trace the development of the game of squash
back to the origins of ball games but it is beyond the scope of

this book to offer anything like a complete history of an exercise so ancient and cosmopolitan. It must suffice to give the briefest of histories on the relationship of squash to other ball-and-racket games.

It is known that in the 13th and 14th centuries the game of tennis (real, royal, or court tennis – whichever you prefer) was played in France as a means of recreation and exercise.

Tennis continued to be played throughout the centuries and was truly called the game of kings; Francois I and Henry VIII were two of the many monarchs who used to play. Rackets developed indirectly from tennis as a ball-and-racket game which could be played by one person hitting a ball against a wall. Apart from Harrow, a version of rackets used to be played by the debtors in Fleet prison.

The game of squash soon developed from the earlier versions of rackets and in about 1860 a Major Harry Gem used to play a game at Leamington which historians claim to be the modern origin of the game of lawn tennis. In 1874 a Major Walter Wingfield patented a game called Sphairistike or Lawn Tennis. There is no doubt that this new game took not only its name from the original game of tennis.

The evolution of any game presupposes a past of considerable duration and although the game we know today as squash is comparatively young in its present form, it has a pedigree as long as most modern games.

13 THE GAME'S ADMINISTRATION

The Squash Rackets Association

The Squash Rackets Association was formed in 1929 to cater for the needs of a growing sport; up until then a sub-committee of the Tennis and Racquets Association had lent some semblance of organisation since its formation in 1907. Also in 1907 the United States Squash Rackets Association was formed to administer their version of the game.

The SRA is the central authority for the game of squash in all matters connected with the organisation and playing of the game with special reference to rules, championships, international matches, disputes, and other such matters. The principal functions of the SRA are to exercise control over the game as well as offering a service to the many affiliated clubs and local authorities with squash facilities. The aspects of control include the rules of the game, sponsorship, public relations, and contact with the Sports Council (often a benefactor in the form of grants).

Clubs can affiliate themselves to the SRA on payment of a fee; in return they can call upon any aspect of the SRA's expanding advisory coaching and technical service. The SRA's experience and expertise in areas of administration, organisation, control, and playing of the game are useful to the majority of clubs.

In addition, clubs may participate in leagues and club competitions, hold important matches or tournaments, hold coaching clinics and exhibitions – and enjoy SRA support in organising events, raising sponsorship, and gaining publicity.

As far as the technical service is concerned, this centres mainly on aspects of court construction, design, materials, and so on. Maintenance and repair also come within the SRA's expert knowledge – and its help can even be sought on planning arrangements and the raising of finance for new centres.

The Women's Squash Rackets Association

The WSRA was formed in 1934 to act as the central authority in all matters connected with women's squash, with special reference to rules, disputes, competitions, and team selection. All open tournaments and championships are held under the jurisdiction of the WSRA, which is affiliated to the SRA.

The International Squash Rackets Federation

The ISRF was formed in 1966 to provide an official world amateur championship. This was at the instigation of the Australian Association, who had grown weary of raising the finance to send their best amateurs halfway round the world to compete in the British Amateur Championships (recognised then as the *de facto* world championships).

Of course, that was not the only reason to form an international body, but there was also a need at that stage to encourage the growth of the game in areas where it did not previously exist. A third object was to have a valid organisation that could settle disputes of an international nature between member nations.

All the world's principal squash-playing nations come under the jurisdiction of the ISRF although many of them have had their own associations for far longer. For instance, Great Britain, USA, Canada, Australia, and New Zealand had associations before the war. Egypt and Pakistan formed associations soon after the war and ever since, participating nations have formed their own associations to conduct domestic affairs.

The European Squash Rackets Federation

Since its formation in 1929 and until 1966, the SRA was acknowledged as the central administrative body for squash throughout the world, apart from the USA. In 1966, the International Federation was formed but continued to use the same offices in London as the SRA. Accordingly, the SRA has been at the forefront of the world development of the international game.

During the past few years the squash boom in Britain has encouraged more interest on the continent and visits to the SRA have become more and more frequent. To foster this increase in potential European development, the European Squash Rackets Federation was formed in April 1973 during the first European Squash Rackets Championship in Edinburgh (to which the SRA invited 10 European nations to send teams).

The Championship was started to stimulate further interest in the game in Europe and the second European Championship was duly held in Sweden in April, 1974. The Championships also provide an excellent opportunity for representatives of national squash interests from the various countries to meet and discuss further development.

The European Federation thus acts as the focal point for the stimulation and development of the game on the continent. At the moment, England and Sweden are able to contribute more in terms of experience but eventually each nation will be able to make contributions of interest to all member countries.

The British Squash Rackets Proprietors Federation

The BSRPF was formed in 1973 to protect and look after the interests of the 'commercial' clubs in Great Britain. It was felt that with the pooling of experience of all commercial court owners, i.e. those who have invested money in facilities for reasons which are other than charitable, the best interests of the owners and the game would be served. The basis of operation of the Federation is to help members to avoid making costly mistakes by introducing them to other members who have already avoided such mistakes, or who have made them and subsequently been able to rectify them.

In other aspects, some of the Federation's services seem to duplicate those of the SRA, i.e. advice on design and construction, which should in any case tend to be a matter of individual preference – it would hardly be desirable to have all squash clubs exactly the same. However, the Federation does also offer advice on how to manage clubs with a particular view to financial efficiency, which is an invaluable service to all would-be developers.

The BSRPF works side-by-side with the SRA in the promotion and development of the game, although there may occasionally be differences of opinion between the two bodies. Basically they do not perform the same function but are complementary to each other.

The Association of Squash Players

In 1974 the leading professionals formed an international association to liaise with governing bodies, tournament promoters, and sponsors, and also to influence the development of professional competition and protect the interests of their members. Ken Hiscoe of Australia and Jonah Barrington of Great Britain were appointed president and chairman respectively.

This new association of the principal actors on the professional stage of the game can be of great benefit to all squash competitors who reach a certain standard.

Part Three

THE PLAYERS

Hashim Khan

Hashim Khan is acknowledged as the greatest squash player ever. His record of 45 major tournament victories which include an unequalled record of seven British Open Championships is testimony to this fact. Perhaps more significant is the indelible impression left with those who saw him at full flight – the impression of unchallengeable mastery.

Still coaching and competing in the USA, Hashim Khan is a legend in his own time, and what is even more astonishing is the fact that he did not compete outside the Indian sub-continent until he was 35!

Born in 1916 at Nawakilla, a village near Peshawar in the North-West Frontier Province of what was then India, Hashim Khan is a Pathan. However, his tribe had come down from the wild Khyber Pass to settle on the plains, and Hashim's father was Chief Steward at the Officers' Club in the British Army's cantonment in Peshawar. There it was that eight-year-old Hashim became a ball-boy for the officers when they hit the ball out of their court, which had no ceiling. Hashim also learned to play by moonlight.

When Hashim was 11, his father died, and from this time his ambition turned to professional squash. He soon gave up schooling to practise by himself for long hours on the squash court. He outgrew the ball-boy service, but waited until he was 28 before being able to take up professional squash coaching. He was appointed coach to the British Air Force in Peshawar.

Hashim Khan first received recognition as a champion when he defeated Abdul Bari in the final of the All-of-India championships held in Bombay. Bari, a cousin, hailed from the village of Nawakilla, but the two had not seen each other since childhood. Hashim's first of three triumphs in this event over Bari was in 1944. It was the former's first match on a court with timbered floors and he was playing before a large gallery, also a new experience. In spite of weighing only eight stone, Hashim quickly returned Bari's renowned drop shots and repeatedly caught him flat-footed.

Only the sub-continent partition and independence problems could halt Hashim's dominance of this event. In 1949, at a time when he was coach to the Royal Pakistani Air Force, he won the inaugural Pakistan Professional Championship from the 21-year-old Roshan Khan, a distant relation, who was destined to follow Hashim to British Open eminence.

When Bari declined an invitation to play for Pakistan, the High Commissioner enquired for another squash player to bring honour to the young nation. The diplomatic corps and the Air Force hierarchy knew little of Hashim's talents, and it was a close call that he was asked to represent the country in the British Open Championships against the formidable world leader Mahmoud-el-Karim. Karim, the Egyptian professional, was deemed to be the perfect squash player by virtue of his elegant stroking and decade of unbeaten matches.

Hashim Khan, however, demolished the seemingly invincible Karim with sheer weight of shot and pace of foot. The squat, barrel-chested, spindly-legged Hashim ran the tall, languid Egyptian (at 30, five years his junior) ragged. On his return to Pakistan he was heaped with accolades, and even the schools were closed for a day! In 1951 he defeated Karim again in the British Open; later in the same year he toured Australia and New Zealand.

Hashim's style of play was originally based on the speed with which he could return an opponent's stroke and the accuracy of that return. Usually his shots were low and hard, forcing errors from his opponents. But his eye for the ball left none of his opponents in any doubt that had he needed any great range of shots, he could have acquired them. Indeed in successive years when he returned to Britain to win the Open, he improved his stroke-making by displaying a powerful and uncannily severe nick-shot played across the court. His ball control was such that whereas for other players a low, hard drive barely above the tin was an attacking shot, to him it was merely another 'safe' one.

He won with commensurate ease wherever he went, presiding over the squash world until the vagaries of age caught up with the heavy demands exacted by the international style of squash. It was logical that Hashim then turned his hand to the North American style of the game with less emphasis on fitness, plus a greater financial return for his immense skills

Hashim Khan not only dominated the world during his international playing years, but led, and influenced, the complete national hegemony that Pakistan experienced in global squash competition through their other champions, Azam, Roshan, Mohibullah, and latterly Sharif in North America.

Younger brother Azam, a tennis coach, was persuaded by Hashim to pursue squash, and with close association and training, succeeded Hashim to win four British Open Championships. Roshan Khan from the same 'stable' joined them and Mohibullah Khan, a nephew of all three, became the last of the Khans to take the British Open title, in 1962. As Hashim moved to Detroit, so followed his eldest son Sharif, as did Mohibullah, to set about establishing a new dynasty in the USA.

Hashim Khan has carved a legend in record books around the world as a squash player without peer, and as leader of a nation that ruled the squash world for over a decade.

Jonah Barrington

Jonah Barrington has been the most influential personality in European squash since he burst into the headlines in 1966 by being crowned both British Amateur and Open Champion in the same season.

The impetus given to the growth of squash by the media stemmed largely from the endeavours of Barrington and the style in which he carried them out. In short, he was news. At a time when British world champions were becoming increasingly difficult to find, Barrington sustained his winning form to take every major championship in the world with the exception of the World Amateur. At 35 (in 1974), Barrington has annexed the British Open no less than six times, and stands only one victory short of the great Hashim Khan's record of seven triumphs. For only the second time in eight years, Barrington recently failed in his attempt on the title. He was bundled out of the championship by Mohammed Yasin, who played his heart out in the Pakistani crusade to keep Hashim's record alive.

It was not the first set-back that Barrington has suffered. He developed his tremendous tenacity during his childhood in Cornwall, trying to overcome the natural advantage that an older brother holds in competitive play, and life in general.

Schooling at Cheltenham did little to make the young Jonah feel at peace with the world. His time spent at Trinity College, Dublin, proved to be thoroughly enjoyable from a self-indulgent point of view, but soon it was quite clear that the aimless Barrington was in need of some salvation. This he found in squash; it put meaning into his life, giving him new purpose and a code of behaviour.

Nazrullah and Azam Khan, two remarkable Pakistani professionals, were instrumental in this process. They gave Barrington the inspiration and guidance to tear through the ranks of squash players who stood between him and his goal – to be the best in the world.

To gain the attention of the squash kingdom and the Press, Barrington had to knock the reigning world champion, Abou Taleb of Egypt, from his perch, and subdue the redoubtable amateur, Aftab Jawaid of Pakistan. Once installed at the top, Jonah then had to prove time and again, before hundreds of different galleries, that he was truly the ruling monarch. He had globe-trotted as an amateur, but on tour with Taleb, Sharif Khan, Rainer Ratinac of Australia, and Jawaid, playing exhibitions around the world, Barrington notched up further Open titles in Australia, Egypt, and Pakistan.

It has not all been plain sailing for the champion, however. Every opponent delights in playing his best against a champion, and there were even those who refused to admit the position he held until recently. They were chiefly the three Australians, Hunt, Hiscoe, and Nancarrow. An edge in fitness has often enabled him to overcome Hiscoe, but for a number of years the lanky Nancarrow spelt trouble for Barrington. Both being left-handers, and Nancarrow, as ungainly as his shots were deceptive, created a nightmare for the Cornishman. Two of Barrington's major ambitions were frustrated by Nancarrow – the 1967 World Amateur title, and the 1969 British Open.

The threat posed by him no longer looms so large since the series staged in 1973-74 around Britain, during which the two contested a professional 15-match tournament. Barrington won by the slightest of margins, but it was enough to put paid to the bogey. The series was an innovation of Barrington's when he first brought Geoff Hunt from Australia to play in a similar contest in 1970.

Hunt, as Barrington's successor to the British Open crown, has been the ever-present threat to the latter's world dominance. He won the 1970 series 13-2, but Barrington retained the Open. Whenever the two met on courts favourable to attacking driving, Hunt would be favourite to win the encounter. But if the air was warm and the walls offered little help to power squash, i.e. it was a slow court, then Barrington could lob his way to victory, albeit in matches which consistently lasted more than an hour and a half. This was testimony to the incredible amount of training that was to capture the attention of the Press in Barrington's early reign, the training which today continues to consume large slices of Barrington's life. Famous are the Barrington excursions to Central Africa, to find peace, sun, and altitude training.

Apart from the rigours of physical training, and Barrington's famous pain barriers which he crashes through *en route* to major titles, many hours have been spent labouring away in squash courts in search of the hallmark of the really magnificent player; ball control. Ball control, even after two torrid hours of squash, was what Barrington had to have if he was to defeat Hunt; so that was what he acquired.

Often criticised for not being a natural stroke player but for simply gaining his titles by retrieving powers, Barrington is grossly underestimated. It is true that he does not have a complete range of finishing shots, for example he has difficulty in dealing with short ground strokes, but the accuracy of placement that he shows in pushing the ball into the back of the court, taking it from any speed, and being able to keep it there, has been the downfall of every opponent at some time in his career.

Barrington's tactics of burying his opponent in the corners of the court, forcing errors or weak returns to be killed with a small, deceptive array of short shots, and running him off his feet, are executed with precision. Always challenging for the centre of the court to dominate proceedings, Barrington is content to win in the end, and so is not perturbed if he loses the first game and a half without scoring himself – just as long as his opponent has become weary for the next phase of the game, when Barrington takes over the ascendancy.

Barrington has scored some memorable victories over Hunt in this fashion. His economy of swing helps his tactics. Not only does he try not to introduce a margin for error in his short, abrupt swing of the racket, but he also saves the energy which is vital in the fifth set. This factor was crucial to his last British Open triumph over Hunt in 1972 when the Australian stood two points away from the crown, but had been drained of the strength to even stroke the ball correctly. Barrington swept through the last few points from behind to take the championship by the slightest advantage in stamina. Barrington's grip on world squash has slipped for the time being, although the loquacious professional is preparing a campaign to re-establish his position.

Apart from the impact he has made on the record books of squash, his immeasurable benefit to the popularising of the sport in Britain with the stamp of his personality, and the cause of the professional player rising under his leadership, make him the catalyst of squash development in Britain over the past decade.

Geoffrey Hunt
Geoff Hunt is the foremost exponent of power squash and currently the world's leading player.

He has disputed Barrington's reign as world champion since 1967, but had only once won the British Open, acknowledged as the ultimate championship, until 1974.

From Melbourne, Australia, Hunt took up squash at the age of 12. His father Vic is an astute judge of squash, and was a pillar of administration in the boom period of Australian squash. He influenced Geoff's style and tactics with what he had learnt from Dardir and the Khans. The result, as witnessed in Hunt's style today, is unique, although it has the basic trade marks of orthodoxy. There is nothing fanciful or particularly radical in Hunt's style, although he swings the racket up to a third more than normal, and hits the ball in a much flatter trajectory.

His technique is to rain a barrage of stinging drives on his opponent, sweeping him wide to the back corners of the court, as he himself constructs the game from centre-court. By using his special athletic prowess and lightning eye, he volleys as much as possible, forcing his opponent to play shot after shot, in quicker and quicker succession. Then, when the opponent is sagging in the back corners, Hunt angles the ball, making him rush forward. Hunt must then cover the next shot at top speed, because he is aiming to hit it to length before his opponent can recover. And so it goes on – relentless pressure, with drop shots and powerful nicks to finish off any stray balls. Hunt's speed of eye, mind, and foot enable him to retrieve a multitude of shots which, against anyone else, might have been winners.

Opponents who do not attempt to play their own shots end up trapped into playing Hunt at his own game – a fatal mistake. The only style of play which has on occasion beaten him is the kind used by Barrington and Alauddin on 'slow' courts, where they lob remorselessly high to Hunt's backhand. This keeps the ball out of the danger of being hit into the nick, forces Hunt on to the defensive and prolongs the rallies. By attacking, they hope to cadge sufficient mistakes to outlast Hunt, provided that they themselves can play error-free squash. But Hunt has countered such strategy by becoming fitter, so that he can beat them at their own game. Zatopek-style 400-metre sprinting is a feature of his training, which clearly succeeded in making him the undisputed number one player in the action-packed British tournament circuit in 1973.

Four times Australian Amateur, thrice World Amateur, and British Amateur Champion, Hunt has won innumerable titles both before and after turning professional late in 1971. At 27 he has many years ahead of him in which to reap the financial harvest of the growing professional circuit, if his successes in South Africa, Australia, and Britain are any indication.

Off-court, Hunt is a quiet, pleasant man. He gave up his scientific interests – he has a BSc in chemistry – for squash. Although none of his family have been able to match his brilliance on the squash court, his brother, sister, and father have all been leading exponents of the sport in both home-state Victoria, and national (Australian) spheres.

The power and speed with which the dynamic Hunt demonstrates his skills is an attractive showcase for the sport, when he is not faced with the negative tactics of some close rivals. Then the match battle tends to become a question of whether the appalling onslaughts of his attacking style can overwhelm the dull constraints of persistent lobbing.

Gogi Alauddin

Gogi Alauddin is today the leader of the legion of Pakistan players performing in world-class squash. The diminutive Gogi is served well by a cool head and incisive mind; although physically slight, on court he combines great speed and balance with subtle stoke-play, governed by great determination.

Despite his off-court friendliness and good-natured cheeky humour, his squash tactics are chilling. Facing bigger, stronger opponents full of power squash, Alauddin sets about wearing them down, humbling them by remembering his squash professional father's advice – 'use brain, side-wall, lob, and drop'. It is this unobtrusive style that has reduced every player in the world at some stage. Although the major prize of the British Open has as yet eluded Alauddin (once a finalist and twice a semi-finalist), he has collected scores of titles, competing regularly in Europe for the past four seasons.

From Lahore, Gogi Alauddin rose through junior squash ranks with close friends Hiddy Jehan and Sajjad Muneer. He won various titles in the Punjab, and the Pakistan junior title; in 1967, at the tender age of 17, he represented Pakistan at the first World Amateur Championships in Sydney and Melbourne, Australia. That was the beginning of Gogi's extensive touring, although he missed almost certain selection for the same event in 1971, held in New Zealand, due to the internal squash politics at that time.

In London the following year, Alauddin pulled off his first major success outside Pakistan by winning the British Amateur championship title, from the position of sixth seed, to defeat unseeded Bill Reedman of Australia. Alauddin extinguished Reedman's fight in a typical show of 'counter-punching'; if Reedman hit hard, Gogi hit softly; from a straight drop shot he would counter with a crosscourt drop softly falling into a dead nick.

The following year he won again, this time defeating Egyptian Mo Asran in five hard-fought sets. Alauddin was having an off-day on the hot Bruce Court at the Lansdowne Club,

Mayfair, but even so exhausted Asran. Alauddin's infinite patience and tenacity enabled him to direct the pattern of play, without finding his finishing form, and he eventually carried the day. Riding on the glory of two Amateur triumphs, Alauddin announced his professional intentions and set about notching up victories over the Open élite.

His first match against Hunt was a disaster. On the same court where weeks before he had achieved his crowning amateur glory, Hunt's power swept the slight, bewildered Pakistani aside, giving him only four points as a memento. This presented a challenge to Alauddin, who prepared his game to accommodate Hunt's style. Today, Alauddin stands only second to Hunt in world ranking, and whenever the champion is less than 100 per cent on form, then the tenacious Alauddin is eager to chase the current champion – and beat him. The training Alauddin undergoes is strenuous, but geared to his physical ability. It is basically of a speed, agility, and stamina-building nature. As professional squash includes more and more tournaments, month after month, players of slight stature, relying on the containing strategy, will need all the stamina they can muster to counteract the master stroking of their rivals.

Gogi follows a 'softening-up' strategy to begin his matches, by running his opponent about the court without trying to hit outright winners. The rallies become prolonged by these tactics thus offering no mistakes on which his opponent can capitalise. The latter begins to feel the strain physically and tries to strike winners, more often than not failing to do so. Alauddin's speed copes with all but the best of shots, and at this point, having run his opponent into the ground and nullified most of his desperate shots, he is now in a position to toy with his opponent much like a cat playing with a mouse.

Alauddin's stroke-play is much less disciplined. He is no puritan in shot-making – but the effect is all, no matter the means. Consequently his wrist droops, his legs and feet are planted with expediency rather than style foremost in his mind; only the racket face angle is important, for its effect on the trajectory of the ball. Invariably when under pressure, Alauddin hits the ball high on to the front wall to lob it deep down the court. This shot will give him time to recover his position in the centre of the court, and afford potential dominance of the rally.

Alauddin is always thinking, always probing a weakness to exploit. He has the advantage of youth in his contention for the title of World Champion, although he must be wary of his budding young fellow countrymen, Zaman and Mohibullah.

Hiddy Jehan

Hidayat (Hiddy) Jehan is a hope for the future of professional squash. In a period of victory based on fitness, the timely intrusion of a daring shot-maker is a welcome relief.

A generous extrovert, Jehan enjoys life in general and squash in particular. Son of a squash professional in Quetta, Pakistan, Jehan sought to improve his game in Lahore, training with Alauddin and Muneer. As Alauddin captured the British Amateur titles, it was Jehan who was his sole serious contender in Europe. With the Australians absent, only Jehan was able to defeat friend Alauddin; this he managed in the Welsh Amateur and West Wycombe events, where Alauddin over-played his defensive tactics and failed to take the opportunities presented to him.

Jehan, a popular player, was held back from reaching the summit in world rankings by his own impetuous nature, which led him into stroking errors when attempting just one too many breath-taking winners. His impetuosity also led him to express his frustration over controversial refereeing decisions, thereby losing the necessary concentration to win evenly-contested matches.

He turned professional after losing to fellow-countryman Mohibullah in the semi-finals of the 1973 British Amateur Championship. It was a memorable match – Jehan played in a masterly fashion, reaching match-ball in the fourth game only to succumb in a full five sets to the relentless retrieving of young Mohibullah, who went on to win the title. Since then Jehan has reversed the decision and settled the score for that season. Throughout the 1974 Open circuit of tournaments he went from strength to strength, establishing himself as the number four player in the world. What is more significant is the style in which he has gained the ranking, and the potential talent still untapped in that style which could carry him further up the rankings.

Strongly built, Jehan thumps the ball with searing drives,

119

especially across-court from the forehand. His versatility is amazing, both with overhead and ground strokes. One reason for this is his obvious enjoyment in their success, and another, on a more practical level, is the incredible strength he possesses in his right wrist. He can turn a drop shot into a drive with a flick of the wrist, hence adding attack and accuracy to deception – a potent mixture in a player who thrives on success.

Greater success is promised as Jehan matures mentally and tempers his stroke-play. He is cast in the die of Hiscoe – that of an attacking player – and is thus a squash player who wants to win off his own inventive racket. At the age of 24, Jehan has the touch of the master to lead the squash world. He has had his set-backs – such as the railway accident which nearly cost him his life in 1967, and certainly his place in the Pakistan team for the World Championships; his allegiance to friend Sajjad Muneer in 1971, whereby he forfeited his position in the team to New Zealand in a political wrangle with internal officialdom; a bout of malaria that caused his withdrawal from the 1972 British Amateur Championship when seeded number two; as well as several crucial defeats at vital stages of his career. In 1969 he found Saleem a stumbling-block. He passed him, but has recently found Zaman and Mohibullah irksome at critical matches in the Pakistan and British Amateur Championships respectively.

Jehan's progress is in his own hands. To harness his brilliance so that none may rival him is his aim, to the delight of galleries who appreciate the gusto with which squash can be played.

Ken Hiscoe

Ken Hiscoe, known as 'The Bear' throughout international squash circles, is one of the most important figures of recent times. He was the first Australian to break on to the world amateur scene with his victory in the British Amateur Championship in 1962. That year heralded the end of British dominance over Australia, ushering in a new style in competitive squash. Hiscoe was the epitome of that attacking, forthright style. The main feature of this school of thought was to volley, volley, volley, thereby pressuring your opponent and moving him or her out of position: 'Play squash as if there are only three walls to the court; if there is no back wall you have to volley.'

If the 1960s saw the emergence of Australian amateur squash, then the powerhouse of that strength shifted from Melbourne to Sydney. Initially, Cheadle, Parmenter, and Binns followed by Hiscoe, Carter, Nancarrow, and Hamilton held sway within Australia whilst providing the nucleus for international representation.

Mixing severe drives to solid length with taxing boasts from the rear of the court to rush the opponent forwards, Hiscoe set up the finishing shots for which he is renowned. His volleying is supreme, either executed directly down the side wall and short, or across court into the nick. A player with a large frame, he crouches in the centre of the court, and powers his volleys short and accurately. His attack also features fine ground strokes. He is keen to play for outright winners; crisp, tight drives down the side walls or delicate drop-shots amidst the heavy artillery of his drives. His achievements, including British, Scottish, South African, and four Australian amateur titles, have been brought about by his desire to defeat his opponents, rather than wage a battle of attrition or play upon weaknesses. He likes to create the opportunities to play for winners, and then hit them. It is this *penchant* for attack, coupled with a fluent, balanced style that makes him one of the world's greatest strikers of the ball and most sought-after exhibition players, despite the onset of back trouble.

Towards the end of 1971, he turned professional with Geoff Hunt and has followed the tournament circuits since, interspersed with exhibitions which have taken the Australian pair across North America, to the Caribbean, Sweden, the British Isles, and Southern Africa. A former captain of the Australian amateur team which has been undefeated since 1962, and former vice-president of the Australian SRA, Hiscoe has been one of the energetic forces symbolising the squash boom in Australia throughout the 1960s.

Cameron Nancarrow

Cam Nancarrow is a tall, lanky, ungainly squash player from Sydney. At 28, he is settling into his new-found professional life with assurance, being ranked number three in the world in

121

1974. Quiet off-court, and awkward on, Nancarrow nevertheless exhibits fire and flare in his squash when it is demanded of
him.

Early in 1972, Nancarrow set himself three personal ambitions to achieve before turning professional and putting to an
end a successful amateur career. He wanted to add the British,
Australian, and World Amateur Championships to his considerable list of achievements. He won all three in due course, but
lost the subsequent 1973 Australian Amateur final to Qamar
Zaman of Pakistan, which must have detracted from his personal assessment of his progress. When he clinched both the
National and World Amateur titles in South Africa, in the same
year, he must have felt relieved that he had realised a burning
ambition. Twice thwarted in the finals of the World Amateur
by Geoff Hunt, Nancarrow finally capped a distinguished
amateur career, both individually and team-wise. Playing for
Australia he won every contest he attempted in four world team
events over six years.

He turned professional late in 1973 to the chagrin of certain
sections of Australian officialdom, and now relishes the
freedom from the burden of the administrators.

Nancarrow is an individualist. His squash is soundly based
along the lines of orthodox Australian attack, but his finishing
shots are certainly original. A left-hander, he plays a host of
drop shots, angles, and nicks to great effect. His height, movement, unusual strokes, and left-handed squash add up to frequent mid-court entanglements with opponents.

His most notable wrangles have been with fellow left-hander
Jonah Barrington, with reference to whom Nancarrow once
held the nickname of the 'Jonah Jinx'. Just as Hunt was to
thwart Nancarrow's hoped for achievements in many events, so
Cam was to intrude into Barrington's plans to capture several
major titles, including a chance to win the 1967 World Amateur
Championship and the 1969 British Open title.

Nancarrow has been involved in squash court owning and
managing for much of the past decade, although he does not
believe that working in squash courts necessarily adds up to a
career in playing the game.

A long-standing rival of fellow Sydney-sider Ken Hiscoe,
Nancarrow has recently held the upper hand in their encoun-

ters, despite an upset in the 1973 Australian Open. Later that year he narrowly lost a 15-match series with Jonah Barrington around England for a purse of £1,250. The series was settled on a 15th game battle in which the first blood to be let was Barrington's, though the Cornishman eventually gained victory in both the match and the series, helping in the process to disprove the 'Jonah Jinx' theory.

A remarkable, quiet, yet fierce determination may once again revive the title, as Nancarrow's game seems to draw tighter, become more efficient, and more deceptive as a result of constant competition. His wife, Mavis, is one of Australia's leading women's representatives, making a formidable husband and wife combination.

Sajjad Muneer

Sajjad Muneer holds distinction as a squash player apart from his undoubted academic ability. Of today's leading Pakistani players, Muneer, with his BSc in Civil Engineering, is the only one with an alternative career to follow. He is still an amateur, and his game reflects this distinction. His old friends and rivals from Lahore, Gogi Alauddin and Hiddy Jehan, have both dedicated themselves to their squash, and reaped the benefits according to their efforts, ranking numbers two and four respectively in the world today. Sajjad ranks lower in the leading 10 players, but this reflects more on his diversity of interests than on his ability.

He was born in the Punjab in 1950, and encouraged by his father to play squash at an early age; in 1961, he was involved in the Punjab Association coaching scheme. His style is easy on the eye, for he seems to flow over the court, executing his strokes with a straight back. His swing is fluent and orthodox, without excess or flounce; and from that swing flows a stream of well-struck drives – straight, crosscourt, and angles from either flank. In short, he is an exemplary squash player.

In constant battle with Alauddin, Muneer won the West Pakistan junior championship in 1964 and 1966, and first appeared in the British Amateur in the 1969-70 season. He has not been beaten by an Englishman since 1971, and in British circles even Barrington has had tremendous tussles before edging home to victory.

The time Muneer devotes to squash may determine his future success in the sport. The 1973-74 season saw a revival of interest and fitness which enabled him to extend himself in competition with the assembled open élite in Britain.

Sajjad's use of the side-wall is crucial in his continued defiance of the English challenge, as Bryan Patterson painfully found out on several occasions throughout that season. Time and again the rhythm and the pattern of the match was altered at Muneer's command, and weak flanks were exposed to be drilled by low, piercing drives. However, Muneer finds it more difficult to establish control against the world's top professionals.

Muneer's interests outside the squash court continue to vie for his attention, so that his squash career is in the balance at an early age. Meanwhile, all but the leading handful must continue to strive to contain this successful exponent of the drive and angle mix.

Heather McKay

It was said that no one would be able to match Janet Morgan's record of a decade's supremacy in women's squash – for she (now Mrs Shardlow) reigned from 1949 until 1958. But after only two years, a bright young star emerged from Australia to upset all the odds and prove absolutely invincible from the day of her first triumph in the Women's Squash Rackets Association Championship in 1961. And now in 1974, Heather McKay, 32, is still as unrivalled as ever. Not only has she been undefeated for these past 13 years, but the margins by which she has defeated every threat to her position are awesome. Winning the WSRA Championship final in about 20 minutes for the loss of only three or four points is about par for the course that Heather McKay has set herself.

Her career has been one of isolation – so far is she in the lead. Her closest rivals, particularly Fran Marshall of England, and Jenny Irving and Marion Jackman (née Hawcroft) both of Australia, have been great competitors, but all have failed to close the gap to make real inroads into Mrs McKay's security of tenure at the top. On a rare occasion Mrs McKay has dropped a single set in a match, but over the span of 13 years the number of these could be counted on one hand.

Heather McKay's motivation is pure and simple. She enjoys playing squash, and whilst she does, she wants to do it as well as she possibly can. So it is because she is a perfectionist that she was driven to train as avidly as she did at first, and that drives her to win by the largest margin she can, always. Her continued success is one of the truly remarkable athletic feats of our age, and her style, apart from her strength of character and will power, is a key factor in this success.

For much of her life she had lived in either Queenbyan or Canberra, Australia, while competing for New South Wales at inter-Australian events. Her techniques have been fashioned from Sydney, revealing a potent forehand, as well as all the basic tactics employed by that school of thought. Her squash is free from eccentricities and frivolous strokes. The emphasis is on sound footwork made possible by fitness and stamina. The footwork aids the shot production and balance, from which comes the power in the driving to the back of the court. Her disciplined use of angles and short shots moves her opponent around the court until finally a space is made and she can slam a drive into it, clearly out of reach of her harassed opponent. By positioning herself in the centre of the court and being ready to strike the ball early, and then powerfully imparting speed to the ball, Mrs McKay builds up pressure on her opponents until the barrage causes a loose shot which is severely dealt with – either by a drive into an unguarded sector of the court, or by crisp short angles and drops.

Although she has only recently turned professional, Heather's life in the past has tended to revolve around the squash court. With her husband Brian, a teaching professional, she has managed squash courts, and played exhibitions throughout the world. Now, with Brian, she holds exhibitions and coaching clinics (when not running a squash club) in their new 'home' city of Brisbane. But squash has not been a totally consuming passion, for Heather McKay has also been active on the hockey field, once again wearing her national colours.

Although her days of representing Australia at squash are over since turning to the professional ranks, nothing seems likely to be able to put a halt to the winning way of the incredible, quiet woman who was beating the world's next best just as easily some 13 years ago as she does now. She has outplayed her generation, and today teaches her future rivals, the up-and-coming youngsters. Although she limits her horizons to playing until the end of the next season, her real constraint will be the time for which squash playing will be satisfying. Heather McKay will then be able to step down from her throne and pass on the crown she most modestly wears, letting her followers try as they may to live up to the Everest-like standards set for them – just as Heather did for her predecessor.

British Players
After the decline of the British amateur squash empire in the early 1960s, it was not possible to revive the supremacy, even with Barrington spear-heading the nation.

Mike Corby, one of the country's greatest sportsmen, was a part of Britain's amateur challenge, and on two occasions ran second to Barrington in the amateur final. After the Irishman turned professional, Corby took over the reins of the nation's squash. A man of flair and personality, his individualism did not always meet with the approval of officialdom, but on court his ability was not to be denied. An extremely gifted player, his style was bright and speedy, though he produced a dogged fighting spirit when it was needed.

He ran the gauntlet of dispute with the administrators, and although still playing international class squash sporadically, he has in effect brought a premature close to his national representation. By being omitted from a touring team to South Africa over an issue of discipline, Corby lost the natural place he held in the British side.

On the South African tour that Corby missed, **Philip Ayton** made his name by winning the South African amateur title. It was the turning point in his career. Since then Ayton (who hails from Brighton, plays for Sussex, but lives in London) has been the leading British squash player until recently. With a tall lean frame, the genial Ayton lobs, drops, and angles with precision and determination. He is renowned for being a slow starter in match play, and finishing all the better in closely-fought affrays of a domestic nature. He is an amateur player with a full time vocation, and consequently his squash suffers from a lack of penetration against the top professionals; but this shortcoming is partly attributable too to his style of play which can be severe, but lacks the knock-out punch necessary to beat the hyper-efficient professionals.

In 1973-74, as mounting pressures affected Ayton, he was toppled from his leading domestic position. **Stuart Courtney**, a gifted left-hander from Dulwich, applied his talents over two seasons to challenge for, and take over, the number one ranking in England and Britain. He confirmed this rating by beating Ayton in the final of the initial British Closed Amateur Championship late in 1973. Courtney, 25, had a distinguished junior career, winning the Drysdale Cup in 1966-67. Other sports also claimed his attention, chiefly cricket and Eton Fives – squash was just another game for him at first. Spurred by the fact that he could not realise his talents while unfit, Courtney trained, claimed a disputed English cap, then played for Great Britain against South Africa at home and in the 1973 World Championships in Johannesburg and Durban. He played in the number three position, behind John Easter and Ayton. He then finished in 1974 ranked as number one, although operating a family business in Cardiff obviously created training and competitive problems. Like Ayton, his amateurism is a restraining feature in the development of his talents.

Two of his British colleagues have sought to realise their squash ambitions in recent times. They are the new professionals, **John Easter** and **Bryan Patterson**.

Patterson, after a successful junior career – Drysdale Cup winner – remained in the north of England and Midlands where his squash progress was stifled. Drawn against Jonah Barrington in a tournament in 1971, he was duly beaten, and the scoreboard depressed him immensely. After long conversations with the champion, he decided to train, train, train. Bomber Harris, ex-PT instructor with the RAF, was the man who made Patterson fit; and it was this new-found fitness combined with strength and determination that took Patterson from number 20 in SRA rankings, to the English team and the 1973 World Amateur Championships. Being number four in this British team left him with time to practise and train while actually in South Africa for the World Amateur, and after several solid individual performances, he created upset after upset by defeating three seeds in the individual championship. He outplayed Roland Watson of South Africa, John Easter, and Dave Wright, the number two seed from Australia. Finishing in the limelight, he entered the final of the World Amateur from nowhere. Cam Nancarrow's experience won the day, but British prestige was revived with Patterson's fairy-tale rise. Failing to repeat this giant-felling form in England, he turned professional and was soon to upset Ken Hiscoe in the 1974 British Open.

John Easter, former Oxford Blue in cricket and squash, has dabbled with accountancy exams for several years while developing his squash. A much travelled player, Easter has been a regular feature of British teams since the 1971 World Amateur Championships in New Zealand. In 1973, he played at number one for Britain in the South African staged World Amateur. One of the tallest of international players, Easter has an attractive all-court game. His size and style draw crowds; many years ago his good looks prompted a 'matinee-idol' label, and this, plus the sight of his long mane of hair streaming as he chops and powers his shots from centre court, packs the galleries.

Persistent hip trouble forced Easter out of much of the 1973 season's play, until he turned professional to tour Kenya with Jonah Barrington in early 1974. Fitness and stamina have long been a problem for him when competing at the very highest level. The dedication and fitness derived from preparing for competition with Barrington could give Easter the impetus he needs to forge forwards in British squash.

One of the amateur hopes of British squash is **Peter Verow**. Verow, 21, is a medical student in London. From Barnard Castle School (like friend Patterson), Verow was the outstanding junior player of his time. Unlike many of his predecessors, he matured quickly to take his place high in the senior rankings, earning himself at his tender age a regular position in the English team. Dividing his time between squash and medicine poses a problem; for with his tremendous natural ability and keen eye for the ball, Verow's squash potential could be rewarding. His game needs the discipline and fitness that concentrated training would bring; his slashing nick-shots and delicate drops would be more reliable under fierce pressure if he had more time to devote to them. Nevertheless, Verow's future seems likely to become part of the backbone of tomorrow's British squash teams.

Part Four

THE RULES OF SQUASH RACKETS

The Rules are published by kind permission of The Squash Rackets Association

The Singles Game
As approved by the International Squash Rackets Federation

1   THE GAME, HOW PLAYED   The game of squash rackets is played between two players with standard rackets, with balls bearing the standard mark of the SRA. and in a rectangular court of standard dimensions enclosed on all four sides.

2   THE SCORE   A match shall consist of the best of three or five games at the option of the promoters of the competition. Each game is 9 up: that is to say the player who first wins 9 points wins the game except that, on the score being called 8-all for the first time, hand-out may, if he chooses, before the next service is delivered, set the game to 2, in which case the player who first scores two more points wins the game. Hand-out must in either case clearly indicate his choice to the marker, if any, and to his opponent.

Note to Referees
If hand-out does not make clear his choice before the next service, the referee shall stop play and require him to do so.

3   POINTS, HOW SCORED   Points can only be scored by hand-in. When a player fails to serve or to make a good return in accordance with the rules, his opponent wins the stroke. When hand-in wins a stroke, he scores a point; when hand-out wins a stroke, he becomes hand-in.

4   THE RIGHT TO SERVE   The right to serve first is decided by the spin of a racket. Thereafter the server continues to serve until he loses a stroke, when his opponent becomes the server, and so on throughout the match.

5 SERVICE The ball before being struck shall be thrown in the air and shall not touch the walls or floor. The ball shall be served on to the front wall so that on its return, unless volleyed, it would fall to the floor in the quarter court nearest the back wall and opposite to the server's box from which the service has been delivered.

At the beginning of each game and of each hand, the server may serve from either box, but after scoring a point he shall then serve from the other and so on alternately as long as he remains hand-in or until the end of the game. If the server serves from the wrong box there shall be no penalty and the service shall count as if served from the right box, except that hand-out may, if he does not attempt to take the service, demand that it be served from the other box.

6 GOOD SERVICE A service is good which is not a fault or which does not result in the server serving his hand out in accordance with rule 9. If the server serves one fault he shall serve again.

7 FAULT A service is a fault (unless the server serves his hand out under rule 9):

(a) If the server fails to stand with one foot at least within and not touching the line surrounding the service box (called a foot fault);

(b) If the ball is served on to or below the cut line;

(c) If the ball served first touches the floor on or in front of the short line;

(d) If the ball served first touches the floor in the wrong half court or on the half-court line. (The wrong half court is the left for a service from the left-hand box and the right for a service from the right-hand box.)

8 FAULT, IF TAKEN Hand-out may take a fault. If he attempts to do so, the service thereupon becomes good and the ball continues in play. If he does not attempt to do so, the ball shall cease to be in play provided that, if the ball, before it has bounced twice upon the floor, touches the server or anything he wears or carries, the server shall lose the stroke.

9 SERVING HAND OUT The server serves his hand out and loses the stroke:

(a) If the ball is served on to or below the board or out of court or against any part of the court before the front wall;

(b) If he fails to strike the ball or strikes the ball more than once;

(c) If he serves two consecutive faults;

(d) If the ball before it has bounced twice upon the floor, or has been struck by his opponent touches the server or anything he wears or carries.

10 LET A let is an undecided stroke and the service or rally in respect of which a let is allowed shall not count and the server shall serve again from the same box. A let shall not annul a previous fault.

11 THE PLAY After a good service has been delivered the players return the ball alternately until one or other fails to make a good return or the ball otherwise ceases to be in play in accordance with the rules.

12 GOOD RETURN A return is good if the ball, before it has bounced twice upon the floor, is returned by the striker on to the front wall above the board without touching the floor or any part of the striker's body or clothing, provided the ball is not hit twice or out of court.

Note to Referees
It shall not be considered a good return if the ball touches the board either before or after it hits the front wall.

13 STROKES, HOW WON A player wins a stroke:

(a) Under rule 9;

(b) If his opponent fails to make a good return of the ball in play;

(c) If the ball in play touches the striker or his opponent or anything he wears or carries, except as is otherwise provided by rules 14 and 15.

14 HITTING AN OPPONENT WITH THE BALL If an otherwise good return of the ball has been made, but before reaching the front wall it hits the striker's opponent or his racket or anything he wears or carries, then:

(a) If the ball would have made a good return and would have struck the front wall without first touching any other wall, the striker shall win the stroke, except that, if the striker shall have followed the ball round and so turned before making a stroke, a let shall be allowed;

(b) If the ball would otherwise have made a good return, a let shall be allowed;

(c) If the ball would not have made a good return, the striker shall lose the stroke.

The ball shall cease to be in play, even if it subsequently goes up.

15 FURTHER ATTEMPTS TO HIT THE BALL If the striker strikes at and misses the ball, he may make further attempts to return it. If after being missed, the ball accidentally touches his opponent or his racket or anything he wears or carries, then:

(a) If the striker could otherwise have made a good return, a let shall be allowed;

(b) If the striker could not have made a good return he loses the stroke.

If any such further attempt is successful but the ball before reaching the front wall hits the striker's opponent or his racket or anything he wears or carries, a let shall be allowed and rule 14 (a) shall not apply.

16 APPEALS An appeal may be made against any decision of the marker.

(i) The following rules shall apply to appeals on the service:

(a) No appeal shall be made in respect of foot faults.

(b) No appeal shall be made in respect of the marker's call of 'fault' to the first service.

(c) If the marker calls 'fault' to the second service, the server may appeal and, if the decision is reversed, a let shall be allowed.

(d) If the marker does not call 'fault' or 'out of court' to the second service, hand out may appeal even if he attempts to take the ball, and if the decision is reversed, hand out becomes hand in.

(e) If the marker does not call 'fault' or 'out of court' to the first service hand out may appeal if he makes no attempt to take the ball. If the appeal is disallowed, hand out shall lose the stroke.

(ii) An appeal under rule 12 or 16 (i) (d) shall be made at the end of the rally in which the stroke in dispute has been played.

(iii) In all cases where an appeal for a let is desired, this appeal shall be made by addressing the referee with the words, 'Let, please'.

Play shall thereupon cease until the referee has given his decision.

(iv) No appeal may be made after the delivery of a service for anything that occurred before that service was delivered.

17 FAIR VIEW AND FREEDOM OF STROKE

(a) After making a stroke a player must get out of his opponent's way as much as possible.

If, in the opinion of the referee, a player has not made every effort to do this the referee shall stop play and award a stroke to his opponent.

(b) When a player:

(i) Fails to give his opponent a fair view of the ball,

(Note: a player shall be considered to have had a fair view unless the ball returns too close to his opponent for the player to sight it adequately for the purpose of making a stroke;)

(ii) fails to avoid interfering with, or crowding his opponent in getting to or striking at the ball,

(iii) fails to allow his opponent, as far as his opponent's position allows him, freedom to play the ball to any part of the front wall and to either side wall near the front wall, the referee may on appeal or without waiting for an appeal allow a let; but if in the opinion of the referee a player has not made every effort to comply with these requirements of the rule, the referee shall stop play and award a stroke to his opponent.

Notwithstanding anything contained above, if a player suffers interference from or distraction by his opponent, and in the opinion of the referee, is thus prevented from making a winning return, he shall be awarded the stroke.

Note to Referees

(a) The practice of impeding an opponent's strokes by crowding or by obscuring his view is highly detrimental to the game and referees should have no hesitation in enforcing the penultimate paragraph of this rule.

(b) The words 'interfering with . . . his opponent in getting to . . . the ball' must be interpreted so as to include the case of a player having to wait for an excessive swing of his opponent's racket.

18 LET, WHEN ALLOWED Notwithstanding anything contained in these rules.

(i) A let may be allowed:

(a) If, owing to the position of the striker, his opponent is unable to avoid being touched by the ball before the return is made;

Note to Referees

This rule shall be construed to include the cases of the striker whose position in front of his opponent makes it impossible for the latter to see the ball or who shapes as if to play the ball and changes his mind at the last moment preferring to take the ball off the back wall, the ball in either case hitting the opponent who is between the striker and the back wall. This is not, however, to be taken as conflicting in any way with the referee's duties under rule 17.

(b) If the ball in play touches any article lying in the court;

(c) If the player refrains from hitting the ball owing to a reasonable fear of injuring his opponent;

(d) If the player in the act of striking touches his opponent;

(e) If the referee is asked to decide an appeal and is unable to do so;

(f) If the player drops his racket, calls out or in any other way distracts the attention of his opponent and the referee considers such occurrence to have caused his opponent to lose the stroke.

(ii) A let shall be allowed:

(a) if hand-out is not ready and does not attempt to take the service;

(b) If a ball breaks during play;

(c) If an otherwise good return has been made, but the ball goes out of court on its first bounce;

(d) As provided for by rules 14, 15, 16 (i) (c) and 22.

(iii) Provided always that no let shall be allowed:

(a) In respect of any stroke which a player attempts to make, unless in making the stroke he touches his opponent; except as provided for under rules 18 (ii) (b) and (c) and 15.

(b) Unless the striker could have made a good return.

(iv) Unless an appeal is made by one of the players, no let shall be allowed except where these rules definitely provide for a let, namely rules 14 (a), 14 (b) and 17 and paragraphs (ii) (b) and (c) of rule 18.

19 NEW BALL At any time when the ball is not in actual play a new ball may be substituted by mutual consent of the players or on appeal by either player at the discretion of the referee.

20 KNOCK-UP The referee shall allow to either player or to the two players together for a period of five minutes during the hour preceding the start of a match for knocking up in a court in which a match is to be played. The choice of knocking up first shall be decided by the spin of a racket.

21 PLAY IN A MATCH IS TO BE CONTINUOUS After the first service is delivered, play shall be continuous so far as is practical, provided that at any time play may be suspended owing to bad light or other circumstances beyond the control of the players for such period as the referee shall decide. The referee shall award the match to the opponent of any player who, in his opinion, persists, after due warning, in delaying the play in order to recover his strength or wind, or for any other reason. However, an interval of one minute shall be permitted between games and of two minutes between the fourth and fifth games of a five-games match. A player may leave the court during such intervals, but shall be ready to resume play at the end of the stated time. Should he fail to do so when required by the referee the match shall be awarded to his opponent. In the event of play being suspended for the day, the match shall start afresh, unless both players agree to the contrary.

Note to Referees

A player may not open the door or leave the court other than between games without the referee's permission.

22 DUTIES OF MARKER The game is controlled by the marker, who shall call the play and the score. The server's score is called first. He shall call 'Fault' (Rule 7 (b), (c) and (d)), 'Foot Fault' (Rule 7 (a)), 'Out of court' or 'not up' as the case may be. If in the course of play the marker calls 'not up' or 'out of court' the rally shall cease. If the marker's decision is reversed on appeal a 'let' shall be allowed except that if the marker fails to call a ball 'not up' or 'out of court', and on appeal, it is ruled that such was in fact the case, the stroke shall be awarded accordingly.

Any return shall be considered good unless otherwise called.

If, after the server has served one fault a 'let' is allowed, the marker shall call 'one fault' before the server serves again.

When no referee is appointed, the marker shall exercise all the powers of the referee.

23 THE REFEREE A referee may be appointed, to whom all appeals shall be directed, including appeals from the marker's decisions and calls. He shall not normally interfere with the marker's calling of the game except:

(a) upon appeal by one of the players;

(b) as provided for in Rule 17;

(c) when it is apparent to him that the marker has made a mistake in calling the game.

First Note to Referees

Notwithstanding the above, in the absence of an appeal, if it is evident that the score has been called incorrectly, the referee shall draw the marker's attention to this fact.

Second Note to Referees

When a decision has been made by the referee, he shall announce it to the players, and the marker shall repeat it with the consequent score, e.g. 'let ball', 'no let', or 'point to——'.

24 POWER OF REFEREE IN EXCEPTIONAL CASES The referee has power to order:

(a) A player who has left the court to play on;

(b) A player to leave the court for any reason whatsoever and to award the match to his opponent;

(c) A match to be awarded to a player whose opponent fails to be present in the court within ten minutes of the advertised time of play.

(d) Play to be stopped in order that a player or players may be warned that their conduct on the court is leading to an infringement of the rules.

Note to Referees

A referee should avail himself of this rule as early as possible where one or other of the players is showing a tendency to break the provisions of rule 17.

25 COLOUR OF PLAYERS CLOTHING Players are required to wear white clothing. The referee's decision thereon to be final.

Appendix I: Definitions

Board (Tin) The expression denoting a line, the top edge of which is 19 inches (.483m) from the floor, set out upon the upper edge of a band of resonant material fixed upon the front wall and extending the full width of the court.

Cut Line A line set out upon the front wall, six feet (1.829m) above the floor and extending the full width of the court.

Game Ball The state of the game when the server requires one point to win is said to be 'Game Ball'.

Half-Court Line A line set out upon the floor parallel to the side walls, dividing the back half of the court into two equal parts called right half court and left half court respectively.

Hand-in The player who serves.

Hand-out The player who receives the service.

Hand The period from the time when a player becomes hand-in until he becomes hand-out.

Not-up The expression used to denote that a ball has not been returned above the board in accordance with the rules.

Out of Court The ball is out of court when it touches the front, sides or back of the court above the area prepared for play or passes over any cross bars or other part of the roof of the court. The lines delimiting such area, the lighting equipment and the roof are out of court.

Service Box or Box A delimited area in each half court from within which hand-in serves.

Short Line A line set out upon the floor parallel to and 18 feet (5.486m) from the front wall and extending the full width of the court.

Striker The player whose turn it is to play after the ball has hit the front wall.

Time or **Stop** Expression used by the referee to stop play.

Appendix II: Standard Dimensions of a Singles Court

Length 32 feet (9.75m); Breadth 21 feet (6.40m)

Height to upper edge of cut line on front wall 6 feet (1.83m)

Height to lower edge of front-wall line 15 feet (4.57m)

Height to lower edge of back-wall line 7 feet (2.13m)

Distance to further edge of short line from front wall 18 feet (5.49m)

Height to upper edge of board from ground 19 inches (.48m)

Thickness of board (flat or rounded at top) $\frac{1}{2}$ to 1 inch ($12\frac{1}{2}$ to 25mm)

Height of side-wall line: The diagonal line joining the front-wall line and the back-wall line.

The service boxes shall be entirely enclosed on three sides within the court by lines, the short line forming the side nearest to the front wall, the side wall bounding the fourth side.

The internal dimensions of the service boxes shall be 5ft 3 in (1.601m).

All dimensions in the court shall be measured, where practicable, from the junction of the floor and front wall.

The lines marking the boundaries of the court shall be 2 inches in width (5.0 cm).

In respect of the outer boundary lines on the walls, it is suggested that the plaster should be so shaped as to produce a concave channel along such lines.

The width of other painted lines shall not exceed 2 inches (5.0 cm).

All walls shall be white or near white. The space below the board shall be white. All lines shall be coloured red.

The front wall shall be of composition. The side walls and back wall shall be of wood or of composition.

The floor should be of wood for covered courts and of composition for open courts.

The board and the space below it to the floor and the area above the height of play on the back wall should be constructed of some resonant material.

Appendix III: Dimensions of a Racket

The overall length shall not exceed 27.0 inches or 685mm. The internal stringing area shall not exceed $8\frac{1}{2}$ inches or 215mm in length by $7\frac{1}{4}$ inches or 184 mm in breadth and the framework of the head shall measure not more than 9/16 inch or 14mm across the face by 13/16 inch or 20mm deep.

The framework of the head shall be of wood. The handle shaft shall be made of wood, cane, metal or glass fibre. The grip and foundation may be made of any suitable material.

Appendix IV: Specification for Standard Squash Rackets Balls

The ball must conform to the following:

1 It must weigh not less than 23.3 grammes and not more than 24.6 grammes (approximately 360-380 grains).

2 Its diameter must be not less than 39.5mm and not more than 41.5mm (approximately 1.56 to 1.63 inches).

3 It must have a matt surface finish.

4 It must be of a type specifically approved for championship play by the International Squash Rackets Federation.

The Doubles Game

1 SIDES Sides shall consist of two players each.

2 SCORE Every point won by either side shall add one to its score.

3 GAME The game shall be 15 up. That is, the side which first scores 15 points wins the game, excepting that:

(a) At 13-all the side which first reached the score 13 must elect one of the following before the next serve:

(i) Set to 5 points, making the game 18 points;

(ii) Set to 3 points, making the game 16 points;

(iii) No set, in which case the game remains at 15 points.

(b) At 14-all, provided the score has not been 13-all, the side which first reached the score of 14 must elect one of the following before the next serve:

(i) Set to 3 points, making the game 17 points;

(ii) No set, in which case the game remains at 15 points.

4 MATCH In all tournaments sanctioned by the Association matches shall be for the best three out of five games.

5 SERVER At the start of a match the choice to serve or receive shall be decided by the spin of a racket.

The two partners of a side shall serve in succession, the first retaining his serve until his side has lost a point. When the side has lost the next point, the side shall be declared out and the serve revert to the opponents. On the first serve of every game, however, the 'in' side shall be declared 'out' after it has lost one point only.

The order of serving within a side shall not be changed during the progress of a game.

At the end of a game the side which has won that game shall have the choice of serving or receiving to begin the next game.

6 SERVICE A ball is in play from the moment at which it is delivered in service (unless a fault or a let) and remains in play until the point is decided.

At the beginning of each game and each time a side becomes 'in' the ball shall be served from whichever service box the first server for the side elects and thereafter alternately until the side is 'out' or until the end of the game. If the server serves from the wrong box there shall be no penalty and the service shall count and the play shall proceed as if the box served from was the correct box, except that, if the receiver does not attempt to return the service, he may demand that it be served from the other box, or, if before the receiver attempts to return the service the referee calls a let, the service shall be made from the other box.

The server, until the ball has left the racket from the service, must stand with at least one foot on the floor within and not touching the line surrounding the service box and serve the ball on to the front wall above the cut line and below the out-of-court line before it touches any other part of the court, so that on its rebound (return) it first strikes the floor within, but not touching, the lines of the opposite service court, either before or after touching any other wall or walls within the court. Otherwise it is a fault.

If it be the first fault, the server shall serve again from the same side. If the server makes two consecutive faults, he loses that point.

7 RETURN OF SERVICE AND SUBSEQUENT PLAY

(a) At the beginning of each game each side shall designate one of its players to receive service in the right-hand service court and the other to receive service in the left-hand service court and throughout the course of such game the service must be received by the players so designated.

(b) To make a good return the ball must be struck on the

volley or before it has touched the floor twice and reach the front wall on the fly above the tell-tale and it may touch any wall or walls within the court before or after reaching the front wall.

(c) If the designated receiver fails to make a good return of a good service it is a point for the serving side. If the designated receiver makes a good return of sevice the side shall alternate making returns until one side fails to make a good return. A failure to make a good return is a point for the other side.

(d) A service called a fault may not be played, but the receiver may volley any service which has struck the front wall in accordance with rule 6.

(e) Until the ball has been touched or has hit the floor twice, it may be struck at any number of times by either or both players on a side.

(f) If at any time the ball hits outside the playing surfaces of the court, which includes the ceiling and/or lights or beams, or hits a line marking the playing surfaces of the court (except on the first service, when it is one fault), it is a point against the side so hitting the ball.

8 LET A let is the stopping of play and the playing over of the point. The following are lets which are not definitely covered in other rules and a let shall be called:

(a) If, on the first bounce from the floor, the ball hits on or above the back wall line.

(b) If either player on the striking side is inadvertently hindered by either of his opponents from reaching or striking at the ball.

(c) If, owing to the position of either of his opponents, a player is unable to avoid being touched by a ball.

(d) If either player on the striking side refrains from striking at the ball owing to a reasonable fear of injuring one of his opponents.

(e) If, in the act of striking and before hitting the ball, the striker's racket is touched by either of his opponents or either of their rackets, even though the striker completes the stroke. However, play continues unless the let has been called by the marker. It is the duty of the marker to call a let, immediately stopping the play.

Note to Referees

No let shall be allowed on any strokes a player makes unless:

(i) In the act of striking and before hitting the ball he touches or is touched by one of his opponents or his racket.

(ii) The striker could have made a good return. Each player on the striking side is entitled to make a return so long as the ball is still in play and is entitled to a let within the above definitions even if his partner has struck at the ball and missed it completely or if he himself has struck at the ball and missed it completely, but still has an opportunity to play it.

9 KEEPING OUT OF OPPONENTS' WAY Each player must get out of his opponents' way immediately after he has struck the ball and do all he can to:

(a) Give his opponents a fair view of the ball. However, interference purely with an adversary's vision in following the flight of the ball is no let.

(b) Avoid interfering with either opponent in getting to and/or striking at the ball.

(c) Leave both opponents, as far as possible, free to play the ball to any part of the front wall or to either side wall near the front wall.

10 BAULK If in the opinion of the marker interference with the striker is unnecessary, it shall constitute a baulk. When a baulk is called, the play shall stop and the point go to the side interfered with.

Unnecessary crowding shall constitute a baulk, even though the opposing player is not actually prevented from reaching the ball or striking at it.

It is the duty of the referee to call a baulk, immediately stopping the play.

11 FAIR BALL TOUCHING PLAYERS If a fair ball, after hitting the front wall and before being played again, touches any player or anything he wears or carries, before touching the floor twice, the side of the player touched loses the point.

12 FAIRLY STRUCK BALL HITTING PLAYER

(a) If the ball after being struck from a good service or a good return and before reaching the front wall, hits one of the striker's opponents or his racket or anything he wears or carries:

(i) It shall be a let if the ball strikes the front wall fairly or would have done so but for such interference.

(ii) If the return would not have been good, the striker's side shall lose the point.

(iii) The marker shall decide as to (i) or (ii).

(b) When a fairly struck ball hits the striker's partner, it is a point for the other side.

13 PLAYER'S PRIVILEGE IN CASE OF LET OR BAULK If the marker fails to call a let or baulk, when in the opinion of the player he has been interfered with, the player may appeal to the marker.

14 KNOCK-UP At the request of either side the referee shall allow to either side or to the two sides together a period of five minutes during the hour preceding the start of a match for knocking-up in the court in which a match is to be played. The right to knock-up first shall be decided by the spin of a racket.

15 CONTINUITY OF PLAY Play shall be continuous from the first service until the match is concluded except that between the third and fourth games play may be suspended by any player for a period not to exceed five minutes and except that, when necessitated by circumstances not within the control of the players the marker may suspend play for such period as he may consider necessary. This proviso shall be strictly construed and play shall never be suspended to allow a player to recover his strength or his wind. The marker shall be the sole judge of intentional delay and, after giving warning, he must disqualify the offender.

16 (a) No ball, before or during a match, may be artificially treated; that is, heated or chilled.

(b) At any time when not in actual play another ball may be substituted by the mutual consent of the players or by decision of the marker.

17 REFEREE The referee's decisions on all questions shall be final. The referee has power to order:

(a) A player who has left the court to play on.

(b) A player to leave the court for any reason whatsoever and may award the match to his opponents.

(c) A match to be awarded to a player whose opponent fails to be present in the court within ten minutes of the advertised time of play.

Standard Dimensions of a Doubles Court

Length 45 feet (13.70m): Breadth 25 feet (7.60m)

Height to lower edge of front wall line 20 feet (6.10m)

Height to lower edge of back wall line 7 feet (2.15m)

Distance to further edge of short line from front wall 30 feet (9.15m)

Height to upper edge of cut line on front wall 8 feet 2 inches (2.50m)

Height to upper edge of board from ground 17 inches (0.45m)

Height of side wall line 20 feet (6.10m), extending from the front wall 31 feet (9.4488m) and 15 feet (4.5720m) high from that point to the back wall, a distance of 14 feet (4.2672m).

The service boxes shall be defined by a line in the shape of an arc of a circle, the radius of which shall be 4 feet 6 inches (1.3716m) from the point of intersection of the short line and the side wall, this arc to be drawn from the short line towards the back of the court to meet the side wall.